BECOMING AN AI
ORCHESTRATOR

JON KROHN'S **PEARSON AI**

SIGNATURE SERIES

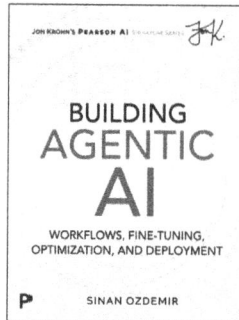

BECOMING AN AI ORCHESTRATOR

A BUSINESS PROFESSIONAL'S GUIDE TO LEADING, CREATING, AND THRIVING IN THE AGE OF INTELLIGENCE

P   SADIE ST LAWRENCE

BUILDING AGENTIC AI

WORKFLOWS, FINE-TUNING, OPTIMIZATION, AND DEPLOYMENT

P   SINAN OZDEMIR

Jon Krohn's Pearson AI Signature Series moves beyond the buzz to offer proven, real-world strategies for the era of artificial intelligence. As the initial excitement around AI gives way to the practical question of "What's next?", this series provides the answers. It equips readers with the expertise to design, manage, and master AI systems that deliver tangible results.

Titles in this series primarily focus on three areas:

1. **Hands-On Engineering:** Roadmaps for deploying production-grade AI

2. **Strategic Orchestration:** Accessible frameworks for enhancing human ingenuity at both the individual and organizational level

3. **Foundational Principles:** The core subjects on top of which modern AI is built

The series aims to connect these three areas, fostering the mindset of an AI builder. Whether you are architecting enterprise systems or guiding your organization through change, these books provide enduring principles that will remain relevant long after the next model is released. The time to build is now. This series provides your blueprint.

Visit **informit.com/awss/krohn** for a complete list of available publications.

》Pearson

informIT®

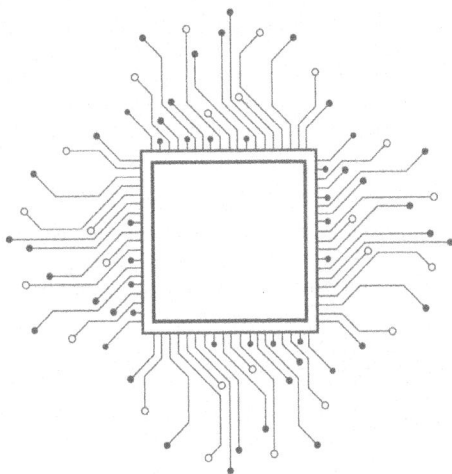

BECOMING AN AI ORCHESTRATOR

A BUSINESS PROFESSIONAL'S GUIDE TO LEADING, CREATING, AND THRIVING IN THE AGE OF INTELLIGENCE

SADIE ST LAWRENCE

ISBN-13: 978-0-13-534463-7
ISBN-10: 0-13-534463-8

4 2026

To the creator within us all, may these pages remind, inspire, and empower you to bring your visions to life.

Contents

About the Author

Sadie St Lawrence is the Founder and CEO of the Human Machine Collaboration Institute (HMCI), where she leads pioneering research, education, and advising efforts aimed at optimizing human and machine interaction in the AI-driven era of knowledge work. She also founded Women in Data™, an international non-profit organization represented in 55 countries with a thriving community of over 70,000 data professionals. Under her leadership, Women in Data was recognized as a Top 50 Leading Non-Profit and the premier community for Women in AI and Tech in 2021.

With academic foundations in piano performance, psychology, and data science, Sadie's career spans from neuroscience research to over a decade leading data science and AI strategy teams at organizations such as VSP and Accenture. Her contributions to the field have earned her recognition as one of DataIQ's Top 100 Most Influential People in Data & AI (2025 & 2024) and Dataleum's Top 30 Women in AI (2022).

Sadie actively contributes to national initiatives as a member of the White House Council for Data and AI Training and the OpenAI Research Community. Her passion for education has driven her to train over 700,000 individuals through data science and AI courses at UC Davis, Coursera, and LinkedIn Learning.

Foreword

We stand at an inflection point in human history. The rise of artificial intelligence isn't just another technological advancement—it represents a fundamental shift in how we work, create, and solve problems. From amongst all the breathless hubbub about this shift, one particular question emerges as paramount: How do we harness AI to amplify human capability rather than replace it?

This book provides the answer.

As host of the world's most listened-to data science podcast, I have welcomed Sadie St Lawrence to my show as the first guest of the year for four years running in order to provide listeners with her invaluable (and near-infallible!) guidance on the AI trends that will shape the future. These forward-looking episodes have been met with rave reviews because of Sadie's unique capacity to distill the firehose of AI-related information down to the most essential, actionable knowledge that will stand the test of time.

With this, her first book, Sadie has greatly expanded upon and deepened her practical guidance for us on collaborating with the AI of today and the AI of tomorrow. Given the tremendous value this work provides, it's my joy and honor to include it as the first title in my *AI Signature Series*.

What sets this book apart is its grounding in Sadie's rich real-world experience. Rather than painting AI adoption with broad strokes, Sadie tangibly demonstrates how curiosity, structured experimentation, and thoughtful integration can transform individual workflows and organizational capabilities. The concept of becoming an "AI Orchestrator"—someone who *conducts* rather than simply *uses* AI tools—represents a fundamental reframing that will resonate with anyone seeking to remain relevant and impactful in the years ahead.

Perhaps most importantly, this book refuses to succumb to either utopian or dystopian visions of our AI-enabled future. Instead, it presents a realistic roadmap for adaptation and growth, acknowledging both the unprecedented opportunities and considerable challenges that lie ahead. The result is a guide that feels both inspiring and grounded, visionary yet practical.

Whether you're a seasoned professional looking to integrate AI into your workflow or a leader seeking to guide your organization through this transformation, you'll find the insights, frameworks, and encouragement you need to not just survive but to thrive in the age of abundant intelligence.

The future belongs to those who can orchestrate it. This book shows you how.

Jon Krohn, PhD,
Series Editor for Pearson's AI Signature Series
New York, September 2025

Preface

From ages 1 to 18, I grew up in a low-tech environment on a quiet farm in southern Iowa. TV, video games, and even CD players were mostly "off-limits" for us kids. I remember when we got our first family computer—an ancient desktop with a boxy screen that was tucked away in a dim, cramped closet in my brother's room. It felt like a treasure trove of possibilities, but time on it was rare and had to be shared. My four older siblings and I would crowd around that glowing screen, practically piling on top of each other, eager to get a turn at the coveted 1995 educational game, *The Oregon Trail*. Even though we had to share, the novelty of exploring even a digital version of the world was exhilarating.

Then, in 1998, a new chapter began: We received a CD in the mail with "America Online" emblazoned on the front. Our curiosity swelled. What was this magical disk promising? After some investigating, we realized it meant our computer needed an "upgrade": It would have to be moved from the closet to the basement, where we could connect it to the phone line. I can still remember the strange symphony of dial-up, the crackle, the whirring, and that final triumphant ping when we finally connected. Waiting for each page to load, line by line, was part of the experience. This was pre-broadband, when patience was a necessary part of going online. Yet even in our rural basement, it felt like a miracle that we could access all this information.

Driven by curiosity, and a desire to avoid sharing with my six siblings, I became obsessed with exploring the Internet on my own. I soon noticed a small detail: The phone line essential for connecting to the Internet ran directly through my brother's room. It became my mission to convince him to swap rooms with me. I began my campaign, extolling the advantages of "better light" and "extra space" in my room. After weeks of persuasion (and maybe some bribery), he finally caved. I had exclusive access at last—or so I thought.

My thrill was quickly dampened when I discovered that my Mac required a specific adapter for dial-up. I couldn't risk letting my parents know about my plan, so I found a way to get it on my own. After some trial and error (and maybe a few nights of frustration), I was connected! For the next few magical months, I could stay up late, secretly messaging friends on MSN Messenger. In my mind, I was the coolest kid on the block, or should I say farm.

These early experiences with technology might seem trivial now, but they represent the beginning of a journey that has shaped my life. Like many of you, I can remember exactly what it felt like to be introduced to technology for the first time. That introduction, whatever it was, often leaves an imprint on us—our "firsts" with computers, the Internet, cell phones, or, for today's generation, artificial intelligence itself. How we meet technology shapes how we relate to it.

Growing up with limited access left me with a curiosity that grew as fast as technology advanced. I spent my nontech hours riding my bike through the fields, playing the piano, and letting my mind wander. In those daydreams, I created worlds.

This book is for the daydreamers and creators, for those who see visions of the future and want to bring them to life. It's my way of sharing the excitement of what's possible, empowering you to navigate this new world of AI, and inviting you to create alongside it.

Introduction

Always evolving, always expanding, always changing—that is the nature of our universe. As humans, however, we tend to cling to the familiar, seeking comfort in routines and the known. When our environment begins to shift, it can be unsettling, yet it's in our nature, and ultimately to our benefit, to adapt. Change isn't just inevitable; it's woven into the fabric of existence.

We often romanticize the past, seeing it through a lens softened by nostalgia. Yes, life may have moved at a slower pace, but it was also marked by limitations. Simple conveniences we take for granted today were hard won or even unheard of a few decades ago. Today, I can connect with people across continents, collaborate with a diverse range of minds, and dive into nearly any topic that piques my curiosity, all in a matter of seconds. I have access to more music, videos, and information than any generation before me could have imagined, with a wealth of knowledge at my fingertips, ready to explore.

However, just as we adjusted to the age of information, we now stand on the precipice of a new era: the age of intelligence. In this era, the vast repositories of data and information we've collected are becoming something more. As they flow into artificial intelligence (AI) systems, they're training machines to learn, adapt, and respond. And just as with every platform shift throughout history, this one will change how we work, live, and play.

For some people, these shifts feel thrilling; for others, they stir anxiety, creating a sense of being left behind or outpaced. That's why I wrote this book. My goal is to help readers understand the forces that have brought us to this point, and to recognize the incredible opportunities, and the important cautions, surrounding this new era. Most importantly, I want to guide you forward, helping you embrace these changes creatively, confidently, and effectively.

Technology has always transformed our lives, but in this age of intelligence, it can be our ally. This book is your roadmap to navigate this new world with curiosity and courage, to work alongside AI, and to find your unique place in a future that promises to be as boundless and evolving as the universe itself.

Who This Book Is For

This book is for creators, knowledge workers, and leaders, as well as for anyone who wants to feel empowered by the new world of work rather than intimidated by it.

- **For Creators:** You're the dreamers and doers, the ones with ideas simmering beneath the surface. Now, more than ever, you have tools and resources within reach to bring those dreams to life. AI is here to expand your possibilities, giving you new ways to shape and manifest your vision.

- **For Knowledge Workers:** You're at the forefront of this shift. Whether you're sorting through data, generating reports, or juggling an ever-changing set of tasks, AI can be the ally that helps you work smarter, not harder. Imagine relieving the stress of repetitive tasks, automating where it makes sense, and reclaiming time for the work that truly matters to you.

- **For Leaders:** The rapid pace of change can be daunting, but with the right understanding, you can navigate it with confidence. This book will help you see through the hype, giving you clarity on how AI is reshaping your team's work and how you can guide them to thrive within this evolving landscape. Whether you're leading a small team or an entire organization, these insights will prepare you to make decisions that shape a positive future.

Making the Most of This Book

To truly benefit from this book, approach it with an open mind and a willingness to try something new.

Neuroplasticity—the brain's ability to adapt and grow—means that no matter your age, you can develop fresh perspectives and skills. But for this growth to happen, you have to first allow yourself to imagine what's possible.

Here's a practical starting point: Engage with the exercises throughout the book. Take time to reflect, envision, and even experiment with different approaches to your work.

Let this book be a space where curiosity leads to discovery.

If you find that a particular section resonates with you, put the book down and explore it further. Yes, it might sound counterintuitive to stop reading, but this book isn't just meant to inform you about theory; it's

also intended to inspire real action. The goal is to help you find what excites you and to fuel that spark of inspiration in your daily life.

Finally, as you read, I hope you'll feel a sense of gratitude for being alive at this pivotal moment in history. With the power of AI at our fingertips, we're uniquely positioned to create, solve, and imagine in ways previous generations could only dream of. May this book empower you to use these tools thoughtfully and boldly, to shape the world you want to live in.

Register your copy of **Becoming An AI Orchestrator** on the InformIT site for convenient access to updates and/or corrections as they become available. To start the registration process, go to informit.com/register and log in or create an account. Enter the product ISBN (**9780135344637**) and click **Submit**.

1

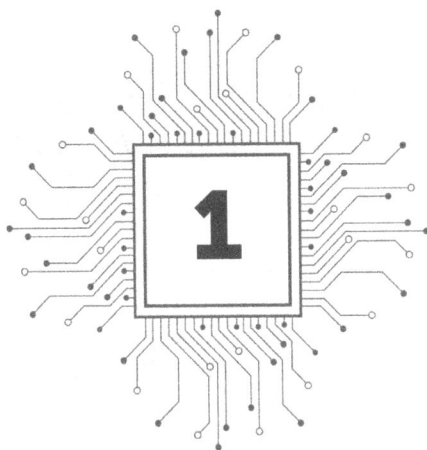

Becoming the Orchestrator

In 2014, I found myself working in the basement of an academic building, conducting research in a neuroscience lab dedicated to understanding emotional learning and memory. It was a windowless, almost dungeon-like space, but I felt a deep sense of purpose. After earning my first degree in piano performance, I had discovered a passion for science that led me here, to studying the mysteries of the human brain. I was proud of myself for making this leap into research, knowing my work could contribute to new insights about humanity.

From Surveys to Synapses: A Journey to AI

My earliest projects in the lab involved designing and analyzing surveys—a seemingly straightforward tool, yet one that quickly taught me a valuable lesson about human nature. We, as humans, are often poor at understanding and accurately reporting on ourselves. Even when asked simple questions, we tend to embellish, distort, or hide the truth to protect our self-image. Thus, surveys, while valuable, have inherent limitations.

This realization led me to a new approach: working with rodents to study fear responses in a more controlled, measurable way. Over several months, I cared for my furry subjects, carefully gathering data on their reactions and behavior. But when the experiment concluded, there was no happy ending. These little creatures wouldn't be set free; instead, it was time to euthanize them and study their brains.

Growing up on a farm, I was no stranger to the realities of life and death; I had butchered chickens and understood the cycle of life. Yet, as I prepared to go through with the procedure, I hesitated. My eyes met those of one of my rodent companions, and in that moment, I knew: This wasn't the path for me.

I left the lab that weekend with a heavy heart, questioning my career path and feeling a pull to make a change. I turned to my usual process for reflection: a pen, a piece of paper, and my computer to help me think through my next steps.

On one side of the paper, I listed everything I loved about my work: science, data, analysis, discovery, coding, and making an impact. On the other side, I noted what I disliked: euthanizing animals, the slow pace of academia, and painstaking data collection. These reflections made one thing clear: I needed a different way to work with data, one that aligned with my values and curiosity.

I typed my list of interests into Google, searching for inspiration. That's when I stumbled upon an article about people leaving academia for a new field called data science.

Data science? The term was unfamiliar, yet intriguing. Data and science, both on my list of passions. But what truly captivated me was the mention of "data scientists" working with algorithms called neural networks. While I had been working tirelessly in the lab, computer scientists were developing ways to replicate the human brain's neural networks with code. My mind raced with the implications: *You mean I could study human behavior not by analyzing brains directly, but through the digital footprints people naturally leave behind?*

That discovery was a revelation. The idea that I could work with artificial neural networks to gain insights into human behavior, without having to study the brain in a traditional sense, ignited something within me. The possibilities felt endless.

That Monday, I quit my lab job, determined to find any opportunity to work with data in the business world. I was ready to dive into this new field and start building my own artificial neural networks.

For the next few years, I immersed myself in learning everything I could about data science. I honed my craft, exploring data, mastering different algorithms, and building models that turned heads. I developed neural network models, created computer vision systems that analyzed retinal scans to predict health outcomes, and crafted marketing models that optimized the flow of products and services. Technologists appreciated the models I built, and business leaders celebrated the results. Still, I could sense that the world wasn't quite ready to fully embrace AI's potential.

The Key That Unlocked It All: Language

In the years I spent perfecting my craft, artificial intelligence (AI) remained mostly a behind-the-scenes tool, something that intrigued technologists but hadn't yet captured the world's imagination. Then, on November 30, 2022, everything changed. Upon its release, ChatGPT became the fastest-growing platform in history, reaching 1 million users in just five days and sparking a global conversation about AI in a way I had never seen before.

For those of us already in the field, ChatGPT's capabilities weren't entirely new. We had seen previous versions like GPT-2 and GPT-3. By the time ChatGPT launched, its underlying language model, GPT-3.5, had become something of a well-kept secret among tech insiders. But this wasn't just another incremental technological leap: It was a breakthrough in how humans and machines could interact.

What set ChatGPT apart wasn't simply the advancement from one model to the next. Instead, the true innovation lay in its conversational interface. Until then, most AI models had worked quietly behind the scenes, enhancing efficiency or making predictions with minimal human input. They reminded me of the Internet in its early, read-only phase, when we would patiently wait for pages to load and passively absorb information that others had created. Back then, the Internet felt like a vast but inert resource—useful, but not interactive (Figure 1.1). It wasn't until social media sparked the read–write revolution that the Internet truly became an integral part of daily life.

The Evolution of a Revolution

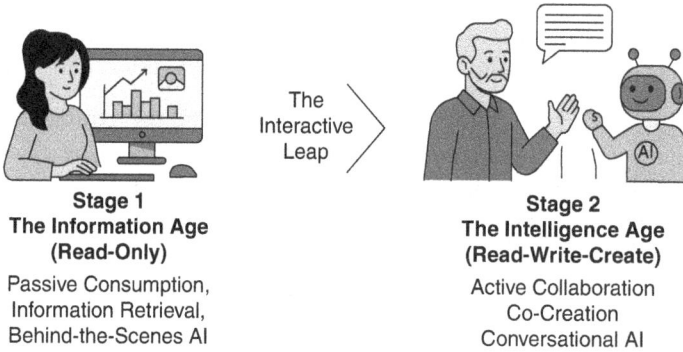

Stage 1 **The Information Age** **(Read-Only)**	Stage 2 **The Intelligence Age** **(Read-Write-Create)**
Passive Consumption, Information Retrieval, Behind-the-Scenes AI	Active Collaboration Co-Creation Conversational AI

FIGURE 1.1 From the Information Age to the Intelligence Age

AI has followed a similar path. Once people could interact with AI through a simple chat interface, a new world of possibilities emerged. For those of us who had nurtured this technology, it felt like watching a child speak its first words. AI had grown from an extraordinary but detached tool into something capable of calling our names, interacting with us, and engaging us in an entirely new way.

> *"There is something particularly human about using tools; the first and most important tool being language."* —Isaac Asimov

For the first time, we had a tool that allowed us to communicate with AI in our most human way: through language. This was a milestone as profound as early humans discovering fire or creating the wheel, a leap that felt both practical and deeply symbolic.

Like many others, I began my new relationship with AI by asking simple questions, wanting to understand its knowledge, see its gaps, and recognize its limitations. I often emerged from my office brimming with excitement, eager to share what I had learned or accomplished through these exchanges with colleagues and friends. It quickly became clear: The way we work is changing, and in my view, it's changing for the better.

The Shift

The more I worked with large language models (LLMs), the more I understood their vast potential and the new ways I could harness their capabilities. To make the most of this technology, I had to rethink not just my workflow, but my entire approach. This shift required me to redefine my role not only as a worker, but also as a creator.

Anyone who has lived through a technological revolution knows this feeling. Those who experienced the dot-com boom, for instance, remember the transformation from manual, paper-based work to having information instantly available. Suddenly, we had an abundance of data, but we still had to sift through it, copy and paste it, and arrange it into meaningful patterns. That access was groundbreaking, yet the work remained labor-intensive.

But with generative artificial intelligence—a form of AI that can create—the nature of work is changing once again. GenAI isn't just a new tool for gathering information: It's a fundamental shift in how we see our roles, our skills, and our potential. I frame this shift as moving from the traditional role to a new role (Figure 1.2).

**The Knowledge Worker's Shift:
From Musician to Orchestrator**

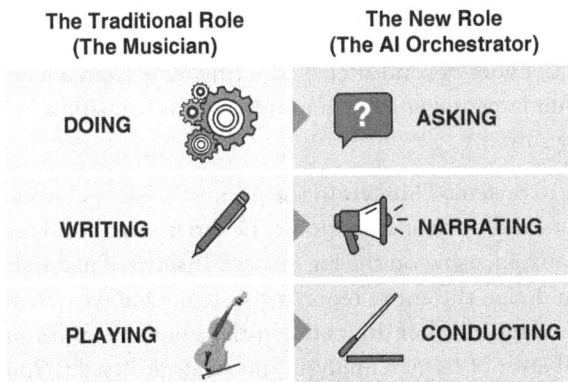

The Traditional Role (The Musician)		The New Role (The AI Orchestrator)
DOING	▶	? ASKING
WRITING	▶	NARRATING
PLAYING	▶	CONDUCTING

FIGURE 1.2 The Evolution of the Knowledge Worker

For those of us who are hyper-curious and brimming with ideas, yet constrained by time and resources, this is a thrilling era. For so long, the scarcity of time has held back our visions. But now, if you are willing to shift from doing to asking, from writing to narrating, and from playing to conducting, you can step into the role of the orchestrator.

Becoming the orchestrator means moving beyond traditional methods to take command of the creative process, guiding it with vision and intent. It's a way to channel your creativity, direct AI's capabilities, and bring ideas to life in ways you might have only dreamed of before.

Becoming an Orchestrator

Traditionally, many of us have operated like musicians in an orchestra. Some of us play the violin, others the cello or trombone. We contribute our individual skills, focusing on our specific parts while following the conductor's lead to create something larger than ourselves.

But with AI by our side, this role is undergoing a profound change. Instead of playing a single instrument, we are becoming the conductor— or, as I prefer to call it, the **Orchestrator**. This transformation marks a shift from hands-on task execution to the art of directing and guiding processes. We are moving from being the musicians to leading the entire symphony.

Why "Orchestrator" instead of "conductor"? A conductor leads the musicians who are already there, but an *orchestrator* arranges the composition itself, deciding which instruments play which parts to create a rich, cohesive sound. This is our new role: not just leading a single process, but skillfully selecting and combining a diverse suite of AI tools to produce a result that is greater than the sum of its parts.

Being an Orchestrator goes beyond simply adopting more than a new title. It requires a fundamental change in mindset. This transition embodies three key shifts:

- **From Task-Doer to Systems-Thinker:** In the past, we were operators, handling the nuts and bolts of execution. The Orchestrator, however, thinks strategically, focusing on the big picture. Instead of just writing a report, you design the entire reporting system: One AI system gathers the latest data, another drafts the initial summary, and you provide the final layer of human analysis and strategic insight. You are no longer just performing a task; you are designing an intelligent workflow.

- **From Answering to Questioning:** A fundamental aspect of this role is the shift from *doing* to *asking*. Where workers were once valued for their ability to execute specific tasks, Orchestrators are valued for their ability to ask the right questions. Their primary skill is identifying key needs and leveraging AI to find innovative answers. This approach prioritizes strategic curiosity over manual repetition, making insight the most valuable asset.

- **From Tool User to Tool Composer:** An Orchestrator doesn't just use one tool; they compose with many. They understand how various AI systems complement each other, when to bring in a new one, and how to tweak the process to solve complex problems. You might use ChatGPT to brainstorm a marketing campaign, Midjourney to generate the visuals, and an automation tool to schedule the posts. In this role, you are no longer bound to individual tasks; instead, you guide a symphony of AI capabilities to achieve optimal results.

This evolution marks the most significant change of all. Historically, AI has been used for simple automation and error correction. But as AI becomes more sophisticated, this relationship is changing. Today's AI tools can challenge assumptions, provoke new thoughts, and even engage in counterarguments. As an Orchestrator, you are no longer just using a tool; you are engaging in an active, dynamic dialogue, fostering a deep cognitive partnership with your digital allies.

Elevating Performance: Bridging the Skills Gap

The integration of AI into the workplace has sparked a remarkable transformation in individual performance. This sea change involves much more than merely automating tasks; it focuses on elevating each employee's capabilities, effectively turning average performers into exceptional ones.

A striking body of evidence suggests that LLMs actually provide the greatest benefits to those with the least experience. In analyses of generative AI rollouts, studies have found these tools are particularly useful for novice and low-skilled workers, helping to bridge skill gaps by disseminating the tacit knowledge that experienced workers already possess. For instance, in writing experiments, participants who initially scored lower showed more improvement when they had access to ChatGPT compared to their higher-scoring peers.

This pattern holds across different fields. A 2023 study by Peng et al. found that the coding assistant GitHub Copilot offered greater benefits to less-experienced developers. Experiments with employees from Boston Consulting Group (BCG) echoed these findings: On consulting tasks, participants in the lower half of the skill distribution saw their performance improve by a remarkable 43%, while those in the top half experienced a more modest 17% increase.

These findings highlight AI's potential to reduce educational and skill disparities in unprecedented ways. By providing a level playing field, this transformation holds the promise of increasing inclusivity and equality, allowing individuals to reach new levels of competency and confidence.

However, this boost in productivity comes with a crucial counterpoint: It doesn't always translate into higher job satisfaction. A study by Aidan Toner-Rodgers, for example, found that 82% of scientists reported a *decrease* in job satisfaction after integrating AI into their work. The reasons were telling: As AI took over many idea-generation tasks, some of the most skilled individuals felt their creativity was stifled and their unique talents underutilized. For them, the efficiency gains of AI came with a trade-off in intrinsic fulfillment, particularly in fields where creative problem solving is deeply valued.

These dual impacts of AI illustrate a vital point. While these tools can elevate performance for many, they can also diminish the personal fulfillment people derive from their work. As AI continues to evolve, balancing productivity with personal engagement will be essential. We must ensure that everyone can thrive not just in terms of output, but also in regard to the joy they find in their work.

A Mindset Shift

The rise of AI offers an unprecedented opportunity to level the playing field, empowering those who previously lacked access to top-tier education or resources. To truly unlock AI's potential, however, we must adjust our mindset. AI isn't just a shiny new tool: It's a smart, capable assistant that can help us achieve goals we may not have imagined were possible. Harnessing this potential requires a shift—from *doing* to *asking*, and from merely executing tasks to orchestrating the flow of work.

Unlike a Google search, where the user types in questions to retrieve static information, interacting with AI is a dynamic process. The aim of this process isn't passively gathering data, but rather co-creating with a responsive partner that can help the user brainstorm, refine ideas, and even think critically. When users engage AI thoughtfully, it becomes a collaborator, helping them approach problems from multiple angles. And just like with any assistant, the quality of the outcomes depends on the quality of the guidance.

A key aspect of this shift is learning to ask strategic questions—an active process that requires both intentionality and skill. I learned this firsthand as the host of the *Data Bytes* podcast. Over the past two years, I've come to appreciate that asking questions is an art. Crafting the *right* question unlocks insights, uncovers nuance, and drives the conversation to a deeper level. Translating this skill to prompting AI was natural, but it took practice.

The principles of a good interview are the same as the principles of effective prompting:

- **Prepare with Intent**
  - **On the Podcast:** For each episode, I study the guest's background to prepare meaningful questions that spark an engaging conversation.
  - **With AI:** This preparation translates into understanding of the basics of your topic or goal. Providing this context allows you to guide the AI toward relevant, high-quality responses.
- **Start Simple, Then Build**
  - **On the Podcast:** Every interview begins with simple, open-ended questions to build rapport and set the stage.
  - **With AI:** Starting with straightforward prompts often leads to richer responses. This allows you to explore topics incrementally and to refine your approach, rather than diving straight into a single, complex query.
- **Listen Actively**
  - **On the Podcast:** I actively listen for unexpected angles or insights that can lead to spontaneous, revealing questions.
  - **With AI:** Take the time to fully read and reflect on the AI's response. This helps you grasp subtleties and identify opportunities to refine your prompts for greater clarity or depth.
- **Dig Deeper**
  - **On the Podcast:** Follow-up questions are what often reveal the core insights I'm looking for.
  - **With AI:** This skill is about refining your prompts based on the initial response. If the answer is too broad, ask for specifics. If it's too shallow, prompt the AI to go deeper. This transforms the interaction from a one-time query into a productive dialogue.

The shift from *doing* to *asking*, or from *playing* to *orchestrating*, begins with mastering this art of the strategic question. This is the key to unlocking

AI's full potential, turning it from a simple tool into a true partner in creativity and problem solving.

Exercise: Enhancing Your Questioning Skills

To practice this mindset shift, try this exercise to refine your questioning skills.

1. **Track Your Questions:** Throughout the day, write down the questions you ask, whether to others, yourself, or an AI system.

2. **Go One Step Deeper:** For each question, identify how you could push it further. What's the natural follow-up? How could you clarify or expand the question to draw out richer insights?

3. **Apply to AI:** The next time you engage with an AI tool, start with a basic question. Then, using your notes, intentionally refine your prompts based on its responses. Observe how different questions lead to vastly different answers.

This practice will help you develop a prompting skillset that turns AI into a powerful collaborator, enhancing your ability to work creatively, strategically, and effectively.

Conclusion

We live in an extraordinary era—one where AI is as close as a conversation away. My own journey, from studying biological intelligence in a neuroscience lab to building AI systems in the business world, is a testament to the power of exploration. It taught me that no matter where you start, curiosity can guide you to new heights. If this new frontier feels intimidating, I hope this chapter has illuminated its vast potential. AI isn't just a tool; it's a collaborator that invites each of us to step into the role of an Orchestrator.

To become an Orchestrator is to embrace this new role with intention. It requires the fundamental shift discussed in this chapter—from *doing* to *asking*, from executing individual tasks to conducting a symphony of digital capabilities. The Orchestrator chooses the instruments, selecting the right AI tool for the right task. They set the tempo, guiding the workflow with strategy and purpose. And most importantly, they provide the interpretation, human insight, creativity, and empathy that transform an output from merely functional to truly meaningful.

But understanding this mindset is only the beginning. To truly lead this symphony, you must learn how to communicate with your new collaborator. The chapters ahead move from the "what" and "why" questions to the "how." They explore the practical art of prompting, unveil the vast array of AI applications that can amplify your work, and introduce ways to navigate the critical ethical considerations of this new age. In these chapters, you will gain the tangible skills needed to not just use AI, but also orchestrate it.

I encourage you to embrace your new role. See AI not as a replacement for your skills, but as a powerful partner in your creative process. As the Orchestrator, you hold the baton. It is your vision that will turn aspirations into achievements, your questions that will bridge ideas into action, and your unique human perspective that will bring it all to life.

2

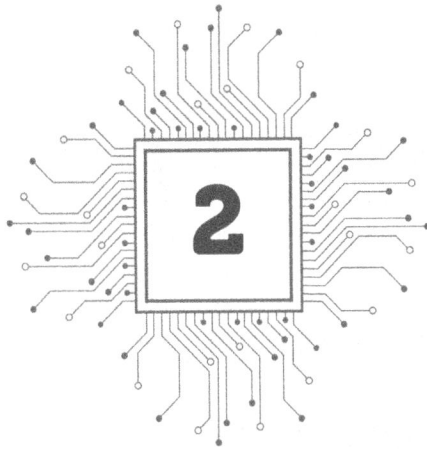

Ask and It Is Given: A Practical Guide to Prompting

When I was a child, I used to imagine having a magical remote control I called a "clicker." This clicker could pause time, rewind moments, and even edit or re-create entire scenarios. But above all, it was a tool for creation. With this clicker in my hands, I could conjure up anything I imagined— new worlds, perfect outcomes, endless possibilities. For years, that clicker remained a whimsical daydream, something I thought belonged only to the realm of fantasy.

That is, until the first time I used ChatGPT. I'll never forget my initial conversation with the model and the sheer joy of seeing its response. It was as if the clicker had come to life. The childlike curiosity, amusement, and wonder I felt in those moments took me right back to the imaginary world of my childhood. Only now, it was real. For the first time, I had a tool that wasn't just capable of following commands, but also could create along with me.

The Rise of Generative AI

For much of its history, artificial intelligence (AI) existed behind the scenes. For the average person, it was largely invisible and often irrelevant to daily life. This situation began to change with the emergence of large language models (LLMs), particularly with widespread exposure to and adoption of tools like ChatGPT. Suddenly, AI wasn't just a back-end technology for businesses or researchers: It was a tool anyone could access, interact with, and use.

Before this shift, the AI landscape was dominated by **discriminative models**. These powerful models have a very specific purpose: to classify and sort data by distinguishing between different categories. They learn to identify patterns and boundaries, essentially saying, "This belongs in category A, and that belongs in category B." Although discriminative models provided huge advantages to organizations, their appeal to the general public remained limited because they answered questions in rigid, predefined ways.

Then **generative AI** entered the scene. Unlike their discriminative counterparts, generative models *create*. They can generate new content, text, images, audio, or even entire datasets, based on patterns they've learned from training data. These models are the creative minds we can collaborate with to co-create.

Table 2.1 summarizes the two different kinds of AI.

TABLE 2.1 Discriminative AI Versus Generative AI	
DISCRIMINATIVE AI	**GENERATIVE AI**
Goal: To classify or sort existing data.	**Goal:** To create new, original content.
Function: Distinguishes between categories (e.g., A versus B).	**Function:** Generates text, images, audio, and more.
Example: A model that identifies whether an email is "spam" or "not spam."	**Example:** A model that writes a new email from scratch.

This shift to generative AI has been a game-changer for knowledge workers. In a digital age where much of the business output involves creating something—whether a report, a design, a piece of code, or a strategy—generative AI expands knowledge workers' capabilities exponentially. It's no longer just about getting the job done; it's about doing it faster, better, and with a level of creativity that often surprises even us.

The Creative Revolution for Knowledge Workers

For knowledge workers, generative AI offers an unprecedented opportunity to enhance their productivity and creativity. Whereas traditional AI models excelled at classification, generative models align perfectly with the core outputs of modern knowledge work. Think about what most knowledge workers produce in a typical day, whether that output takes the form of a written document, an analysis, a presentation, or a design. All of these can now be augmented or even co-created with AI.

What sets generative models apart is their ability to empower us to produce *new* ideas, *new* designs, and *new* solutions. They don't just categorize the past; they help us imagine the future. Generative AI can assist with a wide range of tasks, such as drafting emails, analyzing data, and creating visual materials. It's like having a collaborator who never tires, works at lightning speed, and offers fresh perspectives.

To harness the full potential of generative AI, we need to shift how we think about work and how we engage with this technology.

Generative AI Applications for Knowledge Workers

The rise of generative AI has been a game-changer for knowledge workers. Most of their work output involves some form of creation, whether it's crafting a document, analyzing data, or developing a strategy. What makes generative AI so revolutionary is its ability to co-create alongside its human users, amplifying their creativity, efficiency, and productivity in ways previously unimaginable.

To better understand where AI fits into your workflow, let's examine the core outputs of a knowledge worker. While their tasks vary, they generally fall into ten key categories:

1. **Text: Crafting Documents and Communication** Text is the bedrock of knowledge work, from critical reports and strategic plans to everyday emails and documentation. It's how we communicate complex ideas clearly and effectively.

   • **AI in Action:** Generative AI can draft an entire first-draft report, summarize a long email thread, or generate multiple versions of marketing copy in seconds, giving you the freedom to focus on refinement and strategy.

2. **Data Analysis: Uncovering Insights** Many of us regularly find ourselves working with data in spreadsheets, databases, or dashboards to uncover patterns and inform decisions.

   • **AI in Action:** Instead of inputting complex formulas, you can use natural language to ask an AI assistant like Copilot in Excel to analyze data, identify trends, and create visualizations for you.

3. **Video: Engaging Through Motion** Video has become a cornerstone of modern content, ranging from corporate presentations and educational tutorials to marketing campaigns.

   • **AI in Action:** Tools like Descript allow you to edit video footage simply by editing the text transcript. Meanwhile, platforms like Sora can generate entirely new video clips from a text prompt.

4. **Audio: Communicating Through Sound** Podcasts, lectures, audio guides, and even music are common outputs for knowledge workers in creative, educational, or communication roles.

   • **AI in Action:** AI-powered tools can automatically remove background noise, transcribe speech to text, and even create royalty-free intro music for a podcast.

5. **Software: Building Digital Tools** Developers and engineers create the software applications, tools, and platforms that solve problems and enable others to work more efficiently.

   • **AI in Action:** Coding assistants like GitHub Copilot can suggest lines or entire functions of code, helping developers write, debug, and test software faster.

6. **Design: Visualizing Ideas and Prototypes** Architects, designers, and engineers create sketches, models, and prototypes that are essential for planning and innovation.

   - **AI in Action:** Tools like Midjourney or DALL-E can generate dozens of visual concepts or product mockups in minutes, accelerating the creative brainstorming process.

7. **Educational Materials: Sharing Knowledge** This category includes everything from course syllabi and training modules to interactive e-learning content designed to teach skills and share information.

   - **AI in Action:** An AI tutor can help create a quiz, generate plausible wrong answers for multiple-choice questions, or even design an entire course outline based on a specific topic.

8. **Strategy: Planning and Policymaking** Leadership and management roles require creating the strategic plans, business strategies, and policy documents that guide an organization forward.

   - **AI in Action:** You can use an LLM as a strategic sparring partner to brainstorm ideas, analyze potential market scenarios, and draft initial policy frameworks.

9. **Research: Expanding Knowledge** Academics, scientists, and market researchers produce studies, papers, and books that contribute to our collective body of knowledge.

   - **AI in Action:** Tools like Perplexity.ai can help researchers find and summarize existing literature, identify gaps in the knowledge base, and even draft sections of a research paper with citations.

10. **Social Media: Crafting Digital Content** For professionals in marketing and communications, creating engaging social media posts, stories, and campaigns is a key part of their work.

    - **AI in Action:** AI can generate a week's worth of social media posts tailored to different platforms, suggest relevant hashtags, and analyze engagement data to recommend the best times to post.

Simplifying the Categories

While the list of output categories just presented is comprehensive, it's helpful to simplify them into three primary categories based on how you can leverage AI: **creative**, **analytical**, or a **hybrid** of both. Understanding this framework will help you identify where AI can fit most naturally into your own work (Table 2.2).

TABLE 2.2 GenAI Application Categories

CREATIVE TASKS	ANALYTICAL TASKS	HYBRID TASKS (CREATIVE + ANALYTICAL)
Outputs requiring imagination and originality	*Outputs focused on logic and data-driven problem solving*	*Outputs that blend imagination with structured reasoning*
Video and Audio Production: AI tools can generate scripts, create background music, or edit content.	**Data Analysis:** AI can process large datasets, identify trends, and generate reports.	**Text-Based Content:** AI can draft an article or report (creative), which you then refine with facts and analysis (analytical).
Designs and Prototypes: AI can brainstorm visual concepts, from logos to product mockups.	**Software and Tool Development:** AI assistants can write and debug code, accelerating development cycles.	**Educational Materials:** AI can help design an engaging course module (creative) and generate accurate quiz questions to test knowledge (analytical).
Social Media Content: AI can generate a variety of engaging posts, captions, and images.	**Strategic Plans and Policies:** AI can analyze market data to inform a business strategy.	**Research Papers and Studies:** AI can help find and summarize existing literature (analytical) to inform a new, creative hypothesis.

Why This Framework Matters

Understanding these categories allows you to see that generative AI doesn't just enhance your ability to complete tasks, but rather transforms how you approach them. Tasks that once required hours of focused effort can now be co-created with AI, freeing you to focus on the most strategic and impactful aspects of your work.

For example:

- **Writing Reports:** An AI tool can generate a structured first draft in minutes, to which you then apply your expertise to refine the narrative and add critical human nuance.

- **Analyzing Data:** AI tools can quickly process and visualize large datasets, highlighting trends and outliers you might have otherwise missed, allowing you to focus on interpretation rather than calculation.

- **Creating Videos:** AI tools like Descript enable even novice editors to produce polished, professional-quality content effortlessly, removing technical barriers to creativity.

This simplification doesn't just save time: It unlocks new opportunities. By partnering with AI, knowledge workers can expand their capabilities beyond traditional limits, exploring areas where they previously lacked the skills or resources to succeed.

How I Use AI on a Weekly Basis

To make this tangible, I want to share how I personally use AI every week across the creative, analytical, and hybrid categories of my work. Running multiple companies, creating content, teaching, and conducting research keep me engaged in almost every facet of knowledge work. This broad scope means I'm constantly looking for ways to streamline my processes and expand my creative potential. Generative AI has been my most valuable ally, enabling me to dive into areas I never thought possible.

Creative Augmentation

These are the tasks where I use AI to brainstorm, generate novel ideas, and overcome technical barriers to creation.

- **Video and Audio Production:** Before AI tools became available, video creation felt intimidating due to the technical complexity. Now, a tool like Descript lets me edit video and audio with the same ease as I can edit a text document. This has allowed me to embrace video creation and ensure professional sound quality for my *Data Bytes* podcast, regardless of where I record it.

- **Art and Design:** Even my weekend hobby of abstract painting has been enhanced by AI. Using Midjourney, I can brainstorm and visualize design concepts, helping me explore compositions and color schemes that might otherwise have remained unexplored.

- **Social Media Management:** As someone with dyslexia, writing social media content has always been a challenge for me. ChatGPT has been a game-changer; I can verbalize my thoughts and have this

AI tool help me refine them, improving clarity while staying true to my voice. This collaboration has made the process enjoyable and effective.

Analytical Augmentation

For tasks that are data-driven and require logical precision, I use AI to accelerate analysis and planning.

- **Quick Data Analysis:** I often turn to ChatGPT to converse with datasets. This tool can summarize trends or generate initial code snippets for deeper exploration, streamlining my workflow so I can focus on decision making rather than manual analysis.

- **Software and Technical Planning:** Although I work with a dedicated development team, I occasionally use ChatGPT to draft initial code or project plans. This helps ensure a concept is feasible before I involve the team, saving significant time and resources. In this way, the AI tool acts as a technical collaborator, bridging the gap between an idea and its execution.

Hybrid Augmentation

Many tasks require a blend of both creativity and analysis. In the following areas, AI serves as a partner that can handle initial generation and logical structuring, while I provide the final human insight.

- **Strategic Planning and Policy Writing:** These areas have always seemed daunting to me, but AI has eased the burden. ChatGPT's voice feature acts as an excellent sounding board for strategy discussions. For policy writing, I leverage LLMs to generate first drafts, which I then refine to align with our organization's vision and strategic goals.

- **Educational Materials:** Developing educational content has been transformed. Crafting plausible wrong answers for multiple-choice questions—a task I once found tedious—is now much simpler with AI assistance. However, I still prefer a hands-on approach for drafting class outlines so that I stay deeply connected to the material. For this task, I use AI to support, rather than replace, the critical human touch.

- **Research and Hypothesis Generation:** In the research-focused institute I founded, LLMs are pivotal. They accelerate the research process by helping us explore hypotheses, review existing literature, and draft white papers, allowing me to focus on connecting the disparate insights and driving innovation.

The Future of Work

My extensive use of AI may seem overwhelming, but it offers a glimpse into the future of work. With the help of AI, we're breaking the barriers of what individuals can achieve, expanding our capabilities beyond traditional roles and skillsets.

I don't see myself as special. If anything, my personal AI journey is proof of what's possible. With curiosity and experimentation, anyone can harness AI to do more, be more, and—most importantly—create more. Generative AI invites us to step beyond our perceived limits and explore possibilities that once felt out of reach.

Prompting: The Art of Conversing with AI

One of the most exciting, yet often challenging, aspects of working with generative AI is understanding its vast capabilities. These models can do so much that it's easy to either underutilize them or feel overwhelmed. Where many individuals falter is in failing to push the boundaries of what these tools can achieve. We've grown accustomed to using specific tools for specific tasks: Excel for data, Word for text, Photoshop for design. But what if one tool could assist with all of these tasks? This isn't just a technical shift; it's a psychological one. Breaking work habits requires both intention and practice.

The good news is that interacting with these models doesn't require learning a new coding language. At their core, the new AI tools are designed for natural language conversation. This process of engaging with a model is known as **prompting**. The term is fitting: According to Merriam-Webster, prompting means "to move to action." When we prompt an AI, we're not just giving a command. Instead, we're initiating a dynamic process, asking it to create, analyze, or think critically with us.

The Myth of the "Perfect" Prompt

With the emergence of tools like ChatGPT, the Internet has been flooded with guides for crafting the "perfect" prompt. A survey by researchers from Stanford University and Amazon AI identified more than 29 distinct approaches to prompt engineering, from "chain-of-thought" to "role assignment." While these strategies can be helpful, they can also be overwhelming and, in many cases, unnecessary.

The surprising truth is that complex prompting techniques don't always matter. Research from VMware tested how various prompt-engineering techniques influenced a model's ability to solve grade-school math problems and found the results were inconsistent. The most consistently valuable strategy? Simply *asking the model to improve the prompt itself.*

This finding highlights a simple truth: AI is often better at refining its own instructions than we are.

A Simple Framework: How to Start Conversing with AI

Don't overcomplicate it. The beauty of generative AI is its adaptability. The process mirrors how you communicate with humans: You start a conversation, clarify if needed, and work together to get to the goal. The cost of miscommunication with an AI system is virtually zero, and it's patient, unflappable, and ready to try again.

If you're new to prompting, the best way to get started is to just start talking to the model. Here is a simple, iterative framework to follow:

1. **Start the Conversation:** Begin with a simple, direct request. Ask a question or give it a task, and then observe how the model responds. Don't worry about getting it perfect on the first try. The goal is exploration, not perfection.

    *   **Initial Prompt:** *"Write me a report on climate change."*

2. **Refine with Context:** If the output isn't what you expected, ask again, but add more detail or context. Guide the AI model by specifying the persona, tone, audience, or desired format.

    *   **Refined Prompt:** *"Act as an environmental researcher and draft a report on the impacts of climate change on agriculture, focusing on solutions for small-scale farmers."*

3. **Ask for Help:** If you're still not getting the desired result, ask the model itself for help. This is often the most direct path to a better outcome.

    *   **Asking for Help:** *"How could I phrase this prompt to get a more detailed report with actionable solutions?"*

The beauty of this conversational approach is its flexibility. You don't need to memorize complex frameworks. The more you experiment with this simple cycle of **Start > Refine > Ask for Help**, the more intuitive it will become to guide the model effectively.

An Advanced Prompting Toolkit

You may have seen complex guides online that promise to make you a "prompt engineer" by teaching you dozens of special commands and tricks. A few years ago, when AI models were less sophisticated, these techniques were often necessary to get a decent result.

That era is largely over.

Today's models are designed to understand context and intent much like a human collaborator. The need for rigid, technical prompting has been replaced by the need for clear, thoughtful direction. You don't need to be an engineer; you need to be a good manager. The goal is no longer to "hack" the AI, but rather to guide it.

While a long list of tricks isn't necessary, a few foundational principles of clear communication will always be essential for getting high-quality, reliable results. Think of these not as a complex toolkit, but as the core habits of an effective Orchestrator.

The Orchestrator's Essential Prompting Habits

The essential prompting habits include the following:

1. **Set the Stage with Context and Role:** This is the single most effective way to frame a request. Before you state the task, tell the AI model which perspective to adopt and provide the necessary background. This is the difference between giving an order and briefing a team member.

   Instead of: "*Write a marketing email.*"

   Try This: "*You are a senior marketing manager for a luxury travel brand. Our target audience is high-income individuals older than age 50. Write a short, elegant email announcing our new exclusive tour of the Amalfi Coast.*"

2. **Provide a Clear Definition of "Done":** Don't make the AI model guess what a successful outcome looks like. Be explicit about the format, length, and key elements you expect in the final output.

   Instead of: "*Summarize the attached meeting notes.*"

   Try This: "*Review the attached meeting notes and provide a summary in three distinct parts: (1) a list of key decisions made, (2) a table of action items* *with owners and deadlines, and (3) three open questions that still need to be addressed."*

3. **Use Examples to Demonstrate Style, Not Just Format:** While models are better at inferring format, providing a short example is still the fastest way to align the AI tool to a specific *tone* or *style*. This is especially useful for creative or brand-specific work.

   Instead of: *"Write a social media post in a fun tone."*

   Try This: *"Write a social media post about our new coffee blend. Match this tone: 'Tired of the same old brew? Get ready to blast off with our new Rocket Fuel Roast! #MorningBoost.' Now, use that style for our 'Zen Garden Green Tea.'"*

4. **Iterate and Refine Through Conversation:** The most natural way to prompt is to treat the process like a dialogue. You don't need to get everything perfect in the first prompt. Start with a simple request, see the output, and then provide feedback. Modern AI is built for this kind of back-and-forth.

   Example Follow-up: *"That's a great start, but can you make the tone more professional and add a statistic to back up the second point?"*

With this kind of prompting, the shift is subtle but profound. Prompting is no longer about learning a machine's language, but rather about being exceptionally clear and intentional in your own language. For an Orchestrator, success depends on clearly articulating the vision instead of crafting the perfect technical command. These simple habits ensure that you are always directing the technology, not just reacting to it.

Continuous Learning and Adaptation

One of the most exciting aspects of generative AI is that it's constantly evolving. Each new version of a model brings updates that may enhance certain capabilities while rendering older techniques less effective. In this milieu, staying ahead doesn't mean that you memorize an ever longer list of prompts, but rather that you remain attuned to what suddenly becomes possible.

For example, a year ago, having an AI model analyze a 200-page PDF and cross-reference it with live web data was a fantasy. Today, it's a feature. This doesn't mean you need a new prompting "trick"; it means you can fundamentally rethink the *types of tasks* you can delegate. The question changes from "How do I prompt this?" to "What can I accomplish now that this barrier is gone?"

Prompting isn't a static, technical skill—it's an adaptive, creative one. It grows as you experiment with the expanding frontier of what AI can do.

Exercise: Explore a New Capability

Instead of testing technical prompt variations, this exercise is about exploring a new AI capability to discover its potential. Your goal is to see how a recent advancement can change your workflow.

1. **Choose a New Capability:** Pick one recent AI advancement that interests you.

   Examples: Analyzing a large document (e.g., a 100-plus-page report); creating a short video or presentation from a text prompt; generating and executing code for data analysis; having a real-time, conversational voice chat with an AI.

2. **Design a Mini-Project:** Select a simple, real-world task where you can apply this new capability.

   Example Task (for document analysis): "I want to understand the key findings from my company's latest annual report, but I don't have time to read all 150 pages."

3. **Test the Capability:** Use an AI tool to execute your mini-project. Engage with it conversationally.

   Example Prompt: "Analyze the attached annual report. What were the top three financial highlights, and what were the biggest challenges mentioned in the CEO's letter?"

4. **Reflect on the Outcome:** Did it work? What were the limitations? How could this capability change the way you approach similar tasks in the future? This kind of hands-on exploration is the most effective way to adapt and integrate new AI power into your work as an Orchestrator.

Improving Your Prompts

While these suggestions for prompting are valuable, you might wonder: *How can I gauge my proficiency and measure improvement?* Like any skill, becoming adept at prompting is a process, and I've found that it unfolds in three distinct stages.

The Three Stages of Prompting Proficiency

The three stages of prompting proficiency include the following:

- **Phase 1: Exploratory Stage** In the beginning, you're simply testing the waters. This stage is about experimenting with one or two tools and seeing what they can do. Your prompts might be vague or broad, such as "Draft a LinkedIn post about AI." At this point, the tools aren't fully integrated into your workflow; they're more of an exciting experiment than a daily necessity.

- **Phase 2: Refinement Stage** As you gain confidence, your prompts become more detailed and precise. You start breaking tasks into manageable sections and giving the model clear instructions. For example, in the context of social media, you might outline your content pillars, brainstorm ideas, draft the post, and then use the model to refine the language. Specificity and context become your best friends in this phase, and you begin to see consistent, high-quality results.

- **Phase 3: Integration Stage** In this final stage, AI tools are seamlessly woven into your daily routines. Whether you're crafting reports, analyzing data, or brainstorming creative projects, you instinctively turn to AI as a collaborator. Prompting becomes second nature, and you find yourself working smarter, not harder, across nearly all areas of your work.

Breaking Old Habits

One of the most challenging aspects of prompting isn't applying the technical skill itself, but rather changing your workflow habits. When these models first became available, I placed a sticky note on my computer that simply read, *"Can ChatGPT help?"* It served as a daily reminder to explore how these tools could enhance my tasks. Without that little nudge, I might default to my usual tools and routines.

For example, instead of instinctively turning to familiar search engines like Google, try starting with a tool like Perplexity or ChatGPT. By experimenting with alternative approaches, you create the possibility of new insights and possibilities. Sometimes, the simple act of trying something different can lead to transformative results.

Start with Self-Analysis

Integrating AI tools into your workflow begins with understanding how you spend your time. For more than a decade, I've meticulously tracked my time in 30-minute intervals. Although not everyone needs to be this detailed in their self-analysis, I recommend tracking your activities for at least a week. This exercise reveals your primary tasks and helps you identify opportunities where AI can enhance or streamline your work.

For instance:

- Are you spending hours formatting documents? AI can automate that.
- Are you struggling to come up with creative ideas? AI can provide a jumping-off point.
- Do you dread repetitive data analysis? AI can process it faster and more accurately.

Learning Through Experimentation

The key to improving your prompting skills is experimentation. During the pandemic, I ventured into painting, inspired by the stunning images generated by Midjourney. At first, I struggled to describe my creative visions in words. But after discovering Midjourney's "Describe" function, which helps articulate visual elements, I unlocked a new understanding of art styles and descriptive language. This experience reinforced the value of leveraging documentation and experimenting with new features to grow my skills.

Another way I've honed my prompting abilities is through collaborative learning. At my institute, we often hold "prompt competitions" where teams tackle tasks like creating PowerPoint presentations on specific topics. We then compare outputs, vote on the best, and share the prompts that led to success. These friendly challenges not only foster creativity but also introduce the teams to new tools and techniques.

Original Thoughts Versus AI Assistance

A key strategy in prompting is knowing when to rely on the model for guidance and when to start with your own ideas. Personally, I prefer beginning with a blank canvas and letting my thoughts take shape before I bring in AI to refine or enhance them. However, for some tasks, like brainstorming or outlining, starting with the AI model can be highly effective.

If you choose to lean on AI for creating your outlines or initial drafts, do so intentionally. Be mindful not to use the model as a crutch to mask a lack of understanding. Instead, think of AI as a collaborator, offering suggestions and feedback to strengthen your ideas. By balancing your input with the model's capabilities, you ensure that the final product reflects your unique perspective.

Don't Overthink the Tools

Finally, don't stress over choosing the perfect tool to start with. In my experience, new versions of models often offer only marginal incremental gains for the average user, especially given the rapid pace of AI advancements. The most important step is to start experimenting and adapting as each tool evolves.

Whether you're working with Claude, ChatGPT, or Midjourney, the key is to dive in, explore, and iterate. Over time, you'll not only improve your prompts, but also discover new ways to integrate AI into your workflows, unlocking potential you didn't know existed.

Choosing the Right Tool

The landscape of AI tools is evolving rapidly, with powerful models like OpenAI's ChatGPT, Google's Gemini, and Anthropic's Claude leading the way. These tools excel in core tasks such as text creation, educational materials development, brainstorming, and even some levels of data analysis. Each model has unique strengths. In turn, as a user, choosing the right tool often depends on your specific needs and preferences.

The Rise of Multimodal Models

One of the most exciting advancements is the emergence of multimodal models—that is, tools capable of handling multiple input types, such as text, images, and even audio. ChatGPT, for instance, has already integrated image generation capabilities. In the near future, most models are likely to become multimodal, seamlessly blending capabilities for text, visuals, and more. Imagine creating a presentation where your AI collaborator not only drafts the text but also generates the accompanying visuals.

These developments won't stop at stand-alone tools. Multimodal models are already being integrated into everyday platforms like Microsoft O365, Google Suite, and Adobe Creative Cloud, making them accessible within your daily workflows. This means you won't just be choosing a tool—you'll be enhancing the tools with which you're already familiar.

The Importance of Asking Rather Than Searching

When working with AI tools, one of the most crucial mindset shifts is moving from *searching* to *asking*. For years, we've been conditioned to start tasks with a blank slate, painstakingly piecing together resources and ideas through application of search engines or manual effort. But with AI, the process becomes conversational. Instead of staring at a blank page, you can ask the model to provide a starting point, a draft, or even an entirely new perspective.

This shift is liberating. It allows you to focus on refining and enhancing the outputs rather than expending energy on generating them from scratch. By asking the right questions and providing clear instructions, you can engage the model as a creative partner.

A Trusted Partner in the Making

Working with AI today can feel a bit like collaborating with a new colleague for whom you're learning their strengths, preferences, and quirks. At first, it might take a few tries to communicate your expectations clearly. But over time, as these tools develop memory capabilities and improve contextual understanding, the process will feel more like collaborating with a trusted, long-term partner.

Imagine a colleague who remembers the nuances of your projects, understands your style, and anticipates your needs. That's the direction in which AI is heading. As AI models gain the ability to recall past interactions, they'll become even more intuitive, adapting to your workflows and preferences with remarkable ease.

The Mantra of Prompting

When it comes to working with AI, simplicity is key: *Ask, and you shall receive.* If the output isn't quite right, refine your question, provide more context, or seek assistance. If you're still not satisfied, or if you're curious and want to push the model further, take a moment to explore the tool's reference documentation. These resources often offer valuable insights into advanced features and optimal prompting techniques.

Key Considerations for Choosing Your Tool

Key considerations for choosing your tool include the following:

- **Task-Specific Strengths:** Identify the primary task you need help with—content creation, analysis, brainstorming, or something else—and choose a model that excels in that area.

- **Multimodal Capabilities:** If your work spans multiple formats (text, images, audio), opt for a multimodal tool like ChatGPT or explore emerging platforms with similar features.

- **Integration with Existing Workflows:** Consider tools that integrate seamlessly with platforms you already use, such as Microsoft O365 or Google Suite. This minimizes friction and maximizes productivity.

- **Experimentation and Flexibility:** Don't hesitate to try multiple tools. Each has unique strengths, and experimentation is the best way to discover what works for you.

Conclusion

In this chapter, you've journeyed from the initial spark of curiosity to the practical art of conversing with AI. You've seen how the rise of generative AI marks the beginning of a new era for knowledge workers—one where your ability to create is limited only by your ability to ask. The core lesson is that prompting is not a rigid, technical science; instead, it is a fluid, conversational skill that anyone can develop with practice and an open mind.

The mantra of this new age is simple: *Ask, and it is given.* If the result isn't what you envisioned, you can refine your question, provide more context, or ask the model for help. By moving through the stages of proficiency, from a curious experimenter to an integrated Orchestrator, you can transform AI from a simple tool into a powerful collaborator.

As you begin to apply these techniques, you will find yourself working smarter, not harder. That will free up your time and mental energy to focus on what truly matters: your strategic vision, your creative insights, and your unique human perspective. These are the foundational skills of the AI Orchestrator.

But understanding how to direct these tools is just the first step. To truly lead this symphony, you must also understand the instruments themselves. The next chapter pulls back the curtain to explore what AI is, how it learns, and which key milestones brought the world to this transformative moment.

For now, your call to action is clear: Start asking. Start experimenting. The future of your work is not something that happens *to* you; it is something you will create, one prompt at a time.

3

What Is AI and How Does It Learn?

This chapter asks two questions: "What is AI?" and "How does it learn?" We begin by trying to understand how AI can be defined.

Defining AI

One of the things I find interesting while trying to explain artificial intelligence is that (1) we have no agreed-upon definition and (2) we often use the same word to describe it: intelligence. John McCarthy, who coined the term, defined it as *the science and engineering of making intelligent machines.* That's a lovely definition, but it has one problem: It uses the word *intelligent* (a description) to define *intelligence* (the capacity), essentially looping back on itself.

Other sources try to delve deeper by providing examples. For instance, *The Longman Dictionary* defines AI as "the study of how to make computers do intelligent things that people can do, such as think and make decisions." This definition provides some examples, which is helpful, but it still uses the same word to describe what it is defining. A second problem arises with this definition because the list of tasks that an AI system can perform continues to expand and change. As you might imagine, that makes defining AI extremely difficult.

Exercise: Articulating Your Understanding of Intelligence

To better understand the complexity of intelligence, I found it helpful to reflect on my own intelligence. Here is a quick exercise you can go through to explore and articulate your personal understanding of intelligence and how it manifests in your life.

Step 1. Reflection

- Sit in a quiet place with minimal distractions.
- Close your eyes and take a few deep breaths.
- Reflect on the following questions:
  - What does intelligence mean to you?
  - How do you recognize intelligence in yourself and others?
  - Can you think of a time when you felt particularly intelligent or demonstrated intelligence?

Step 2. Brainstorm

- Take a blank sheet of paper or open a new document on your computer.
- Write down all the words or phrases that come to mind when you think about intelligence. Don't censor yourself; let your thoughts flow freely.

Step 3. Categorization

- Review the words and phrases you wrote during the brainstorming session.
- Group them into categories. For example, you might have categories like "emotional intelligence," "logical intelligence," "creative intelligence," and "practical intelligence."
- Label each category clearly.

Step 4. Personal Definition

- Using the categories and ideas you've identified, write a personal definition of intelligence.

- Your definition should encompass the various aspects of intelligence that you find most meaningful.
- Aim for a paragraph or two.

Step 5. Examples from Your Life

- Think of specific instances in your life where you demonstrated intelligence.
- Write down at least three examples, detailing what you did, how you felt, and why you believe it was an example of intelligence.
- Explain how these examples align with your personal definition of intelligence.

Step 6. Reflection on Growth

- Reflect on how your understanding of intelligence has evolved over time.
- Consider how your experiences have shaped this understanding.
- Write a short paragraph summarizing your reflections.

Sharing and Discussion

If you're comfortable, share your definition and examples with a friend or family member. One of the common insights from this exercise is that it is much harder to define intelligence than you thought it would be. Also, it should become clear that intelligence can take many shapes and forms.

Why Defining Intelligence Matters

Intelligence is a multifaceted concept (Figure 3.1). Intelligence is not just about logic or academic ability; it also encompasses emotional awareness, creativity, adaptability, and more. In addition, our understanding of intelligence continues to evolve.

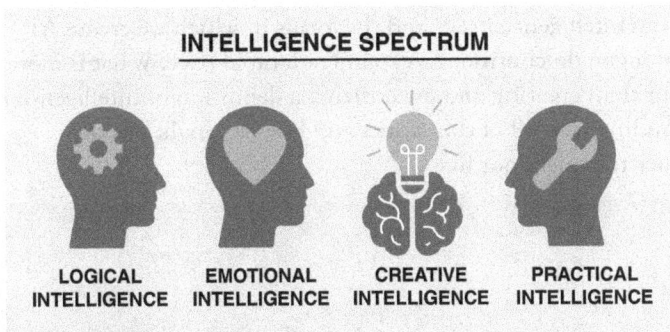

INTELLIGENCE SPECTRUM

LOGICAL INTELLIGENCE   EMOTIONAL INTELLIGENCE   CREATIVE INTELLIGENCE   PRACTICAL INTELLIGENCE

FIGURE 3.1 Types of Intelligence

For example, earlier views on intelligence often held that tool use and complex social behaviors were unique to humans. Observations and studies in the latter half of the 20th century challenged this perspective. Jane Goodall's research on chimpanzees, for instance, revealed that they could make and use tools, demonstrating that tool use was not exclusive to humans. This expanded the definition of intelligence beyond human behaviors, as researchers recognized that many species exhibit sophisticated problem-solving abilities, emotional intelligence, and social structures.

We humans pride ourselves on our intelligence—it is what we believe makes us the dominant species. I also think this is why AI scares some people: If our intelligence is what makes us a dominant species then what happens when we can replicate it? Yet, this challenge also creates an opportunity. As we build AI systems, we uncover new dimensions of intelligence, both artificial and human.

There is a positive side when what we think is innate to ourselves, or part of our own intelligence, such as making and using tools, proves not to be the case. Put simply, we uncover new forms of intelligence and continue to expand our scientific discovery of it.

Our understanding of intelligence continues to evolve,
as does intelligence itself.

As we continue to replicate our own intelligence in machines, the same pattern may occur with humans. That is, we will uncover more of our own unique ways of being "intelligent" and expand our understanding of it, leaving a place and space for all. Rather than fearing what AI might mean for human uniqueness, we can embrace the possibility that it will inspire us to discover new ways of being intelligent.

In summary, defining AI is difficult because we are still working to understand intelligence itself, and the forms in which we create AI and what it can do continue to expand at a rapid pace. What is more important than creating and memorizing a definition of intelligence is understanding how all of this works and how we might use this intelligence to benefit our lives.

AI Timeline: Key Milestones

Understanding AI's journey helps us appreciate how far the field has come and where it's headed. Following is a timeline of pivotal moments in AI history:

- Foundations (1950s–1980s)
  - **1950:** Alan Turing publishes "Computing Machinery and Intelligence," introducing the concept of the Turing Test to evaluate a machine's ability to exhibit intelligent behavior.
  - **1956:** The term *artificial intelligence* is coined at the Dartmouth Conference, where AI is formally recognized as a field of study.
  - **1966:** ELIZA, an early natural language processing program, is created. It simulates a psychotherapist, sparking initial excitement about conversational AI.
  - **1976:** MYCIN, an AI system for medical diagnosis, demonstrates the potential of expert systems.
- Emerging Power (1990s–2010s)
  - **1997:** IBM's Deep Blue defeats world chess champion Garry Kasparov, marking a major milestone in AI's ability to compete with human intelligence.
  - **2011:** IBM's Watson wins *Jeopardy!* against top human players, showcasing advances in natural language processing and information retrieval.
  - **2012:** AlexNet revolutionizes deep learning by using a convolutional neural network (CNN) to achieve breakthrough performance in image recognition.
  - **2016:** Google DeepMind's AlphaGo defeats world champion Go player Lee Sedol—an achievement previously thought decades away due to Go's complexity.
  - **2018:** OpenAI releases GPT-2, demonstrating impressive text generation capabilities and sparking debates about ethical concerns in generative AI.
- AI in Everyday Life (2020s)
  - **2020:** GPT-3, OpenAI's next-generation language model, is released, setting a new standard for natural language understanding and generation.
  - **2022:** ChatGPT is launched, reaching 1 million users in just five days and becoming the fastest-growing application in history.

- **2023:** Multimodal models like OpenAI's DALL-E 2 and Google's Gemini combine text, image, and video generation capabilities, pushing the boundaries of creativity and versatility.

- **2024:** Generative AI moves into productivity suites and enterprise platforms, with Microsoft Copilot, Google Gemini, and Anthropic Claude integrated across email, documents, and workflows. This marks the start of AI as an embedded layer in daily knowledge work.

- **2025:** Autonomous AI agents gain traction, managing complex tasks such as software development, research synthesis, and business operations. The focus shifts from AI as a tool to AI as a collaborative partner, accelerating transformation across industries.

- **Future Horizons**
  - Predictions include AI systems with advanced memory capabilities, more robust autonomy, and wider integration into tools like Microsoft O365, Google Suite, and beyond. These developments promise to redefine productivity and creativity across industries.

Everyday AI

Artificial intelligence is no longer confined to research labs or science fiction; it's deeply integrated into our daily lives. Often, we use AI without even realizing it. These AI-driven technologies work quietly behind the scenes, enhancing experiences, simplifying tasks, and even influencing decisions. Let's explore some common examples of how AI is already a part of your day-to-day routine.

Amazon Recommendations

When shopping on Amazon, you've likely noticed the personalized product suggestions on your homepage or product pages. These recommendations are powered by AI algorithms that analyze your browsing history, your purchase patterns, and even the behavior of other users with similar preferences. By identifying patterns in your data, AI can predict products you're likely to enjoy, making your shopping experience smoother and more personalized.

Social Media Feeds

Platforms like TikTok, Instagram, and Facebook curate your feeds using advanced AI algorithms. These systems analyze your interactions—including what you watch, like, comment on, or share—to understand your preferences and interests. AI then selects content tailored to your tastes, creating a highly engaging (and sometimes addictive) user experience. For creators, this technology also ensures their content reaches the right audience, maximizing engagement.

Facial Recognition

From unlocking your smartphone to enhancing security systems, facial recognition has become a staple of modern technology. AI-powered systems analyze unique features such as the distance between your eyes and the shape of your jawline to verify your identity. These systems learn and improve over time, making them more accurate with every interaction. However, they also raise significant privacy and ethical concerns, highlighting the need for careful oversight.

Language Translation

Tools like Google Translate and DeepL use AI to break down language barriers, enabling seamless communication across cultures. These systems are trained on massive datasets of multilingual text, which enables them to understand context, idioms, and nuanced meanings. Whether translating a foreign menu or facilitating a business meeting, AI can make global communication more accessible than ever.

Exercise: Discovering AI in Your Daily Life

AI is everywhere, but we often overlook its presence because it operates seamlessly in the background. This exercise will help you identify how AI interacts with your daily routines.

Step 1. Reflect on Your Daily Activities

- Think about a typical day. Which tools, apps, or systems do you use regularly? Consider tasks like:
  - Shopping online
  - Browsing social media
  - Communicating via email or chat
  - Navigating with GPS or map apps
  - Watching TV or listening to music
  - Searching for information online
- Write down everything that comes to mind.

Step 2. Identify AI-Powered Tools

- Review your list and mark any tools or systems that might use AI. For example:
  - Does your streaming service recommend movies?
  - Does your GPS suggest the fastest route?
  - Does your email automatically filter spam?
- If you're unsure, do a quick search to confirm whether the tool uses AI.

Step 3. Group by Category

- Organize your AI-powered tools into categories such as the following:
  - Personalization (e.g., recommendations on Netflix or Amazon)
  - Communication (e.g., autocorrect, translation, or chat apps)
  - Navigation (e.g., GPS, ridesharing apps)
  - Security (e.g., facial recognition or password managers)

Step 4. Reflect on Benefits and Concerns

- For each category, ask yourself:
  - How does this tool make my life easier?
  - Are there any privacy or ethical concerns I have about its use?
- Write a few sentences summarizing your thoughts.

Optional: Share and Discuss

Share your findings with a friend, family member, or colleague. Discuss how AI impacts your lives and whether it's something you actively think about or take for granted.

Takeaway

This exercise shows that AI is already a significant part of your daily life. Recognizing these tools helps you appreciate their benefits and fosters awareness of the broader implications of AI in society.

Understanding the AI Effect

Although these systems improve our daily lives, we often fail to recognize them as "intelligent." Tasks such as language translation might seem like clear markers of intelligence, but recommending a product or curating a social media feed doesn't typically come to mind (Figure 3.2).

EVERYDAY AI USE CASES

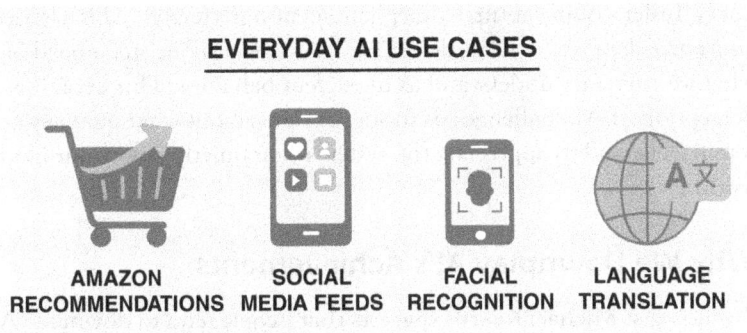

| AMAZON RECOMMENDATIONS | SOCIAL MEDIA FEEDS | FACIAL RECOGNITION | LANGUAGE TRANSLATION |

FIGURE 3.2 Everyday AI

This phenomenon, known as the *AI effect*, was first noted by AI pioneer John McCarthy. McCarthy observed that "as soon as it works, no one calls it AI anymore." In other words, when AI systems become effective and commonplace, they lose their mystique.

Take spellchecking, for example. Once considered a groundbreaking AI application, it's now a standard feature in word processors. Similarly, search engines like Google, which once amazed us with their ability to retrieve relevant information, are now taken for granted. Even defeating a human chess champion—a feat once heralded as a triumph of AI—is no longer seen as particularly special.

Tasks that once seemed like science fiction, such as instant language translation or autonomous vehicles, quickly become mundane once they're part of our daily lives (Figure 3.3). This underscores how our expectations of intelligence evolve over time.

AI'S EVOLUTION FROM NOVEL TO NORMAL

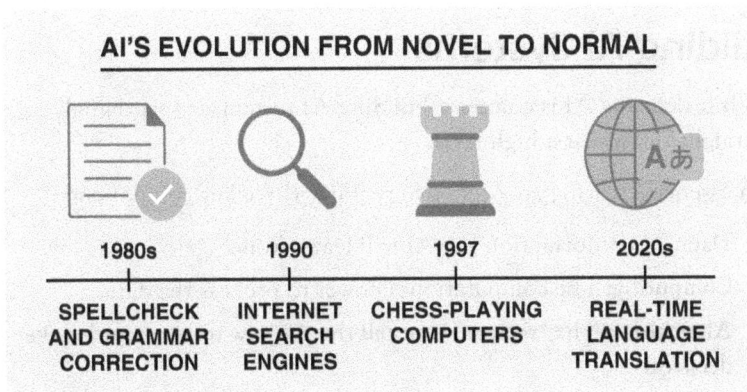

| 1980s | 1990 | 1997 | 2020s |
| SPELLCHECK AND GRAMMAR CORRECTION | INTERNET SEARCH ENGINES | CHESS-PLAYING COMPUTERS | REAL-TIME LANGUAGE TRANSLATION |

FIGURE 3.3 Beginning AI Systems

Larry Tesler's quip captures this phenomenon perfectly: *"AI is whatever hasn't been done yet."* By this definition, AI is always one step ahead of what we currently understand as intelligent behavior. This evolving perception of AI challenges us to stay curious about what qualifies as intelligence and to appreciate the systems that quietly power our modern world.

Why We Downplay AI's Achievements

Psychologist Michael Kearns suggests that people tend to downplay AI's capabilities because we subconsciously want to preserve humans' unique role in the universe. By dismissing AI's achievements as "just technology," we maintain the belief that human intelligence is special and irreplaceable.

But dismissing AI in this way limits our appreciation of its true impact. Recognizing AI's achievements doesn't diminish human intelligence; instead, it highlights our ingenuity in creating systems that enhance our capabilities.

Connecting to the Bigger Picture

The AI effect invites us to rethink our understanding of intelligence. Instead of asking, "What can't AI do?," we should focus on "How can AI empower us?" By embracing AI's capabilities, we open the door to greater creativity, productivity, and innovation.

This perspective sets the stage for the next section, which explores how AI systems are built and the key components that make them work.

Building AI Systems

While defining AI is complex, building AI systems is surprisingly straightforward at a high level.

In essence, creating an AI system requires three key components:

- **Data:** The information the AI will learn from.
- **Computing:** The computational power to process the data.
- **Algorithms:** The "recipes" that tell the AI how to learn and make decisions.

Let's break down each component to understand its role in the AI development process.

Data: The Fuel of AI

Data is the lifeblood of AI. It can take many forms, including the following:

- **Structured Data:** Tabular formats like spreadsheets or time-series data.
- **Unstructured Data:** Text, images, audio, and video.
- **Semi-structured Data:** Formats like JSON or XML.
- **Specialized Data:** Geographic information systems (GIS) or network graphs.

The more diverse and representative the data, the better the AI system can learn. For example, the Internet has provided a vast ocean of text, images, and videos that has fueled recent AI breakthroughs. However, data quality is just as important as quantity, because biased or incomplete data can lead to flawed AI systems.

Computing: The Engine That Drives AI

Computing refers to the hardware and infrastructure needed to process data and run algorithms. In the early days of AI, computational power was a limiting factor. Today, advances in technology have made powerful hardware more accessible. Common components include:

- **Central Processing Units (CPUs):** General-purpose processors.
- **Graphics Processing Units (GPUs):** Ideal for parallel processing, essential for deep learning.
- **Tensor Processing Units (TPUs):** Specialized processors for AI workloads, developed by Google.
- **Quantum Processing Units (QPUs):** Experimental processors that exploit quantum mechanics to tackle certain optimization, simulation, and machine-learning tasks far faster than classical hardware. This technology is still in the early stage of development but is evolving rapidly.

Modern AI systems often rely on cloud-based computing resources, which enable researchers and developers to scale their projects without owning expensive hardware.

Algorithms: The Recipe for Learning

An algorithm is like a recipe that tells a computer how to perform a task. In AI systems, algorithms go beyond static instructions; that is, they enable systems to learn from data and adapt over time. At the heart of this adaptability is machine learning.

Exercise: Build Your Own "AI Recipe"

It's time to think creatively about how you would design an AI system:

1. Choose a task you'd like to automate or improve with AI (e.g., organizing photos, managing emails).

2. Identify the three key components:

   - **Data:** What kind of data would the system need?

   - **Computing:** How much computational power would it require?

   - **Algorithm:** Would it use supervised, unsupervised, or reinforcement learning?

3. Sketch out your AI recipe, considering any potential challenges or ethical implications.

Machine Learning

Machine learning (ML) is a subset of AI that enables systems to improve their performance without being explicitly programmed to do so. ML systems use algorithms to analyze data, identify patterns, and make predictions. There are three main types of machine learning:

- **Supervised Learning**
  - The system learns from labeled data. **Example:** Training a model to recognize plant species using images labeled with their genus.
  - Common use cases: Spam detection, image classification, and predictive analytics.

- **Unsupervised Learning**
  - The system learns from data without labels, finding patterns or clusters. **Example:** Grouping customers based on purchasing behavior.
  - Common use cases: Market segmentation, anomaly detection, and recommendation systems.

- **Reinforcement Learning**
  - The system learns through trial and error, receiving feedback in the form of rewards or penalties.
  - Common use cases: Game-playing AI (e.g., AlphaGo), robotics, and autonomous navigation.

Deep Learning: The Basis of Modern AI

Deep learning is a subset of ML that uses neural networks with multiple layers (hence "deep"). Deep learning owes much of its success to artificial neural networks (ANNs), which are inspired by the structure of the human brain, where neurons transmit signals to process information. While ANNs are not direct replicas of biological neural networks, they borrow the concept of neurons working together to process information.

Let's start with a quick neuroscience primer.

How Biological Neurons Work

Your brain is made up of billions of neurons. Each neuron has three main parts:

- **Dendrites:** Receive signals from other neurons.
- **Nucleus:** Processes the signal and decides whether it's strong enough to pass along.
- **Axon:** Transmits the signal to other neurons if it's strong enough.

When a signal is passed, it's called an *action potential*. In essence, a neuron acts as a simple on/off switch. If the signal is strong enough, it fires.

It's astonishing that these basic components, combined with the brain's intricate network of connections, enable humans to perform complex tasks like recognizing faces, playing instruments, or solving problems.

How Artificial Neurons Work

Artificial neurons mimic the on/off behavior of biological neurons but use digital signals instead of electrical or chemical ones. Here's how they process information:

1. **Inputs:** Digital data (e.g., numbers representing pixel brightness in an image) are fed into the neuron.
2. **Weights:** Each input is multiplied by a weight, which determines its importance.
3. **Summation:** The weighted inputs are added together.
4. **Activation Function:** A mathematical equation decides whether to pass the signal along to the next layer.

The key difference is that artificial neurons use math to make decisions, whereas biological neurons rely on electrical and chemical processes.

Despite this simplification, artificial neurons can approximate complex patterns when connected in large networks.

Components of Neural Networks

A neural network has three main components (Figure 3.4):

- **Input Layer:** Receives the data (e.g., an image or text).
- **Hidden Layers:** Perform computations to identify patterns.
- **Output Layer:** Produces the final result (e.g., "cat" or "dog" for an image).

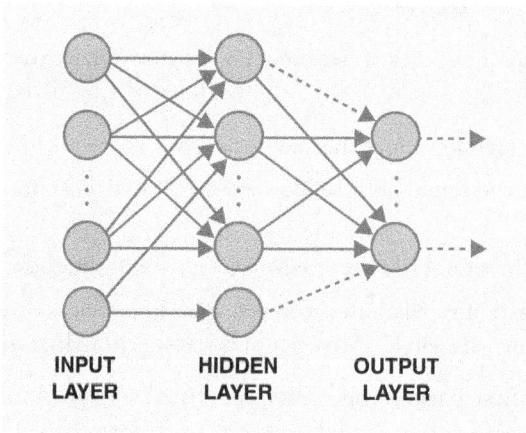

```
INPUT          HIDDEN          OUTPUT
LAYER          LAYER           LAYER
```

FIGURE 3.4 Neural Network Layers

Deep Neural Networks: Layers of Intelligence

A neural network becomes "deep" when it contains two or more hidden layers between the input and output layers. Each layer successively recognizes more complex and abstract features as the information goes deeper into the network.

In computer vision, for example, the process unfolds in a hierarchical way:

- The first layer might specialize in detecting simple features like straight lines at various angles.
- The second layer builds on this by learning to detect combinations of those lines, such as corners, curves, or simple textures.
- Subsequent layers continue to combine these features into even more complex and abstract patterns, eventually allowing the network to identify very specific objects, such as a particular breed of dog, a make of automobile, or a celebrity's face.

By combining information from these multiple layers, deep networks can identify sophisticated patterns and make highly accurate predictions.

Learning in Neural Networks

The magic of neural networks lies in their ability to "learn" by adjusting their weights. This process happens through two key techniques:

- **Backpropagation:** After the network makes a prediction, it compares the result to the actual outcome and calculates the error (the difference between the predicted result and the actual result). This error is propagated backward through the network to adjust the weights.

- **Gradient Descent:** This optimization algorithm fine-tunes the weights by minimizing the error. It's analogous to finding the lowest point in a valley: Each adjustment brings the network closer to the optimal solution.

Over time, these iterative adjustments enable the network to improve its predictions. Backpropagation and gradient descent are discussed in more depth later in this chapter.

Real-World Analogy: Teaching a Neural Network

Imagine you're teaching a child to recognize animals in pictures:

1. You show the child a picture of a cat and tell them, "This is a cat."

2. If they mistakenly call a dog a cat, you correct them and explain why.

3. Over time, the child learns to distinguish cats from dogs based on features such as whiskers, ears, and tail shape.

A neural network learns in a similar way, using labeled examples (in supervised learning) and adjusting its internal parameters until it achieves high accuracy.

Exercise: Neural Network Exploration

A practical thought experiment will help you connect these concepts.

Step 1. Input and Weights

- Imagine designing a neural network to identify handwritten numbers (such as on a check).
  - **Inputs:** What data would the network need (e.g., pixel brightness)?
  - **Weights:** How might certain features (e.g., rounded shapes for "0") carry more weight?

Step 2. Feature Extraction

- Think about how the first hidden layer might detect simple shapes (lines, curves).

- How would subsequent layers combine these shapes into numbers?

Step 3. Reflect

- Write a short paragraph describing how you think a neural network might "see" and learn to recognize numbers.

How Do Neural Networks Learn?

Deep neural networks are so effective because they:

- **Generalize well:** They can apply learned patterns to new, unseen data.

- **Scale with data and computing:** The more data and computational power they have, the better their performance will be.

- **Handle complex tasks:** From image recognition to natural language understanding, neural networks are at the heart of many modern AI breakthroughs.

In essence, deep learning models excel because of their ability to adjust and optimize their internal parameters, like weights and biases, through a process that mimics trial and error. Let's break down these key concepts.

Parameters: The Building Blocks of Learning

In a neural network, **parameters** refer to the weights and biases. Think of weights as the connections between neurons. Stronger weights make it more likely that certain signals will pass through. Biases act as "adjusters," allowing the network to fine-tune its outputs for better accuracy.

For example:

- In an image recognition task, a neuron might assign a higher weight to features like edges or shapes that are important for identifying an object (e.g., a car's wheels).

- Biases help ensure the network can handle cases where the input doesn't match perfectly but is close enough to recognize.

The goal of training is to find the optimal combination of weights and biases that minimizes errors.

Backpropagation: The Key to Learning

Backpropagation is the mechanism that allows neural networks to learn from their mistakes. Here's how it works:

1. **Forward Pass:** Data flows through the network, layer by layer, until it reaches the output layer. The model makes a prediction (e.g., "cat" or "dog").

2. **Error Calculation:** The network compares its prediction to the actual answer and calculates an error using a loss function (e.g., mean squared error for regression or cross-entropy for classification).

3. **Backward Pass:** The error is propagated backward through the network, updating the weights and biases in each layer.

The goal is to adjust the parameters so that the error becomes smaller with each iteration.

Gradient Descent: Optimizing the Path to Accuracy

Gradient descent is an optimization algorithm that fine-tunes the network's parameters. Here's an analogy to help you understand how it works: Imagine you're hiking down a mountain in thick fog. Your goal is to reach the lowest point (the global minimum), but you can see only a short distance ahead. You rely on the slope (gradient) to guide your steps downward.

In a neural network:

- The "mountain" represents the error surface (the higher the error, the steeper the slope is).
- The "steps" represent parameter adjustments.
- The gradient tells the network in which direction to move to minimize error.

This process is repeated iteratively until the model reaches a point where the error is as low as possible.

Variants of Gradient Descent

There are several ways to perform gradient descent, which differ primarily in how much data is used to calculate the error and update the model's parameters:

- **Batch Gradient Descent:** This method uses the *entire dataset* to calculate the gradient and update the parameters in each iteration.

While this provides a very accurate estimate of the gradient, it can be computationally very slow and require a lot of memory, making it impractical for the large datasets used in modern AI.

- **Stochastic Gradient Descent (SGD):** This is a much faster approach. Instead of the entire dataset, SGD uses a small subset of data—a *mini-batch*—to calculate the gradient at each step. In modern practice, the terms "stochastic gradient descent" and "mini-batch gradient descent" are often used interchangeably.

  - **Online Learning:** A special case of SGD where the mini-batch size is just *one data point*. This method is useful when data arrives in a stream, but the updates can be "noisy" or erratic.

  - **Mini-Batch Learning:** The most common approach, which balances the accuracy of batch gradient descent with the speed of online learning by using *small, random batches of data* (e.g., 32, 64, or 128 data points) for each iteration.

Real-World Analogy: Fine-Tuning a Recipe

Think of training a neural network as perfecting a recipe:

1. **Weights and Biases:** Ingredients and their quantities.
2. **Backpropagation:** Tasting the dish and identifying what's off (too salty, not sweet enough).
3. **Gradient Descent:** Adjusting the recipe in small steps (e.g., adding a pinch of salt or a dash of sugar) until it tastes just right.

This iterative process ensures the final result is optimized for accuracy and quality.

Why It Matters

Understanding these concepts isn't just an academic exercise—it's foundational to how modern AI systems operate. Whether you're training a chatbot, developing a self-driving car, or analyzing data, these techniques enable machines to learn, adapt, and improve.

Exercise: Visualize Backpropagation

To deepen understanding, you can visualize the process yourself:

1. Draw a small neural network with three layers (input, hidden, and output).
2. Use arrows to show the forward pass (data flows from left to right).

3. Label an example error at the output layer (e.g., "Prediction: Dog, Actual: Cat").

4. Draw arrows moving backward to represent adjustments to the weights and biases.

Reflect:

- How might small adjustments improve accuracy over time?

- What challenges could arise if the error surface has multiple "valleys" (local minima)?

Key Terms: Building Your AI Vocabulary

Understanding AI requires a grasp of the key terms and concepts within this field. Here are some foundational distinctions that will help you feel confident when engaging in conversations about AI.

Discriminative Versus Generative AI

AI models generally fall into one of two categories: discriminative or generative.

Discriminative Models

These models focus on identifying and distinguishing between different categories.

- **How They Work:** They predict a label or outcome based on input data.

- **Example:** Spam filters that classify emails as "spam" or "not spam."

Generative Models

These models create new data samples and simulate the underlying distribution of the data.

- **How They Work:** They learn the patterns in the data and use this understanding to generate new content.

- **Example:** ChatGPT generating coherent text or DALL-E creating realistic images.

Narrow AI Versus Artificial General Intelligence

AI capabilities vary widely, from highly specialized systems to theoretical models that rival human intelligence.

Narrow AI

- **Definition:** Intelligent systems designed for a single task or domain.
- **Examples:** Speech recognition (like Siri), facial recognition, and recommendation algorithms.
- **Limitation:** Cannot generalize knowledge beyond their specific purpose.

Artificial General Intelligence (AGI)

- **Definition:** A hypothetical AI system capable of human-like understanding and reasoning across multiple domains.
- **Examples:** AGI doesn't yet exist, but it's often depicted in science fiction as robots with human-level intelligence.
- **Potential:** AGI could revolutionize industries but raises ethical and philosophical questions about its impact on humanity.

Large Language Models Versus Multimodal Models

As AI evolves, increasingly more powerful and versatile systems are emerging.

Large Language Models (LLMs)

- **Definition:** AI models that specialize in processing and generating text-based data.
- **Examples:** ChatGPT and Bard.
- **Strengths:** Highly proficient in natural language tasks like summarization, translation, and text generation.

Multimodal Models

- **Definition:** AI systems that can process and generate data across multiple types of media, such as text, images, and audio.
- **Examples:** OpenAI's GPT-4 Vision and Google's Gemini, which combine text and image understanding.
- **Strengths:** Versatility in handling complex, multiple-input tasks, such as describing an image in text or generating visuals from text prompts.

Autonomous Systems

Autonomy in AI refers to systems that can make decisions and perform tasks independently.

* **Definition:** AI systems capable of planning and executing actions to achieve a goal without constant human intervention.
* **Examples:** Self-driving cars navigating traffic or delivery robots moving through busy hallways.
* **Why It Matters:** Autonomous systems are pushing the boundaries of what machines can accomplish, but they also raise questions about safety, ethics, and accountability.

Table 3.1 summarizes these key terms. Mastering these concepts will equip you to engage in informed conversations about AI, whether you're discussing practical applications or exploring the ethical dilemmas of emerging technologies.

TABLE 3.1 AI Vocabulary		
TERM	**DEFINITION**	**EXAMPLE**
Discriminative models	Distinguish between categories	Spam filters, image classifiers
Generative models	Create new data samples	ChatGPT, DALL-E
Narrow AI	Specialized for a single task	Siri, facial recognition
Artificial general intelligence (AGI)	Human-like intelligence across domains	Hypothetical (e.g., sci-fi robots)
Large language models (LLMs)	Text-focused AI systems	ChatGPT, Bard
Multimodal models	Process multiple data types	GPT-4 Vision, Gemini
Autonomous systems	Plan and execute tasks independently	Self-driving cars, delivery robots

Conclusion

In this chapter, you've journeyed through the foundational concepts that underpin AI, exploring its many forms and capabilities. From the elusive definitions of AI to the mechanics of machine learning and neural networks, you've unraveled how these systems learn, adapt, and enhance daily life.

Key Takeaways

Key takeaways from this chapter include the following:

- Intelligence is multifaceted and ever-evolving, making AI both a reflection of human ingenuity and a challenge to our understanding of what it means to be intelligent.

- From personalized shopping recommendations to real-time language translation, AI is deeply integrated into our daily routines, but often goes unnoticed.

- AI systems require data, computing, and algorithms. These building blocks enable machines to learn and perform tasks.

- Inspired by the human brain, the neural networks in AI systems process information through interconnected layers, fine-tuning their weights to achieve remarkable accuracy.

- Understanding distinctions like discriminative versus generative models and LLMs versus multimodal models empowers you to engage with AI on a deeper level.

The Path Ahead

AI isn't just a tool; it's a catalyst for expanding our understanding of intelligence, both artificial and human. As we replicate aspects of our own cognition in machines, we uncover new dimensions of our unique capacities and challenge our assumptions about what makes humans intelligent.

The more we explore AI, the more questions we uncover. This isn't a sign of failure, but rather an indicator of progress. Each new discovery reveals opportunities to create, collaborate, and innovate in ways we've only just begun to imagine.

In the spirit of AI's constant evolution, let this chapter serve as a foundation for your own exploration. The more curious and engaged you are, the more you'll uncover about this transformative technology, and yourself.

Going forward, you'll dive into the practical applications of AI. This exploration will equip you with the tools and strategies to become an Orchestrator in your own right. The journey continues in the next chapter. Let's create together.

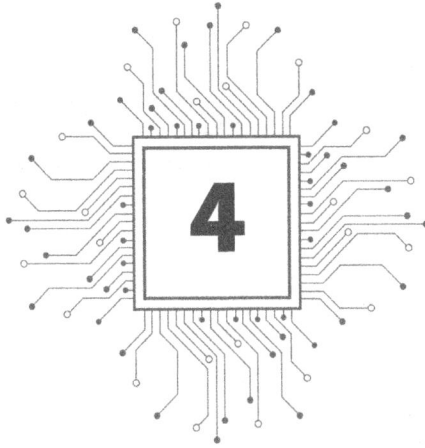

AI Applications

Factors Influencing AI Applications

Potential applications of AI are widespread for two primary reasons: the digitization of business and the drive for productivity gains.

Digitization of Businesses

Over the past two decades, businesses of all sizes have embraced digital tools, laying the groundwork for AI adoption (Figure 4.1). Even a local boutique may use electronic payment systems, online booking platforms, or inventory management software. These digital systems generate data, which is the lifeblood of AI, making businesses inherently ready for AI integration.

Meanwhile, a family-run bakery might use AI to optimize its supply chain, predicting how much flour or sugar is needed based on past sales data. A small fitness studio could leverage AI scheduling tools to improve booking efficiency and manage customer interactions.

While we'll save the robotics discussion for another chapter, the digital landscape today is primed for AI-enhanced workflows.

Digital-to-AI Maturity Curve

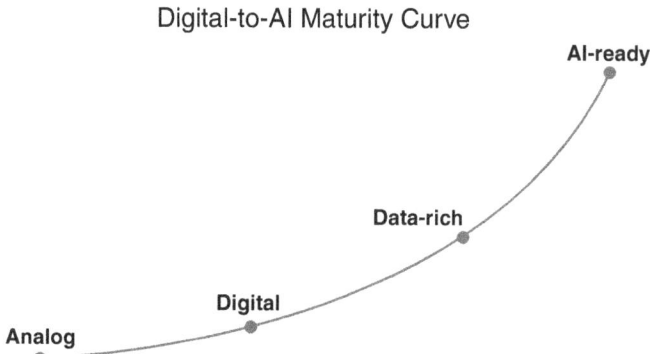

FIGURE 4.1 Business Milestones for Analog to AI

Drive for Productivity Gains

In a capitalistic economy, businesses continuously seek ways to lower their costs and improve their profit margins. AI is a natural fit for this environment, as it offers unparalleled opportunities for productivity improvements and creative problem-solving capabilities. Unlike previous industrial revolutions, in which physical machinery or simple automations served as drivers, this wave is powered by **intelligent systems** that learn and improve with use.

Imagine a small e-commerce store: AI can handle everything from inventory tracking to customer support, while also personalizing product recommendations to increase sales. Furthermore, these benefits can be realized at a fraction of the cost of hiring multiple employees.

The Compounding Effect of AI Technology

This industrial revolution also takes advantage of the **compounding nature** of technology. In previous revolutions, improvements were linear: A better steam engine meant faster trains, for example. But AI builds upon itself. In consequence, each advancement—whether better algorithms, more data, or improved computing power—leads to exponential growth. The more an AI system is used and the more data it gathers, the smarter it becomes.

AI models don't just execute tasks. Rather, they adapt, evolve, and optimize their outputs over time. This ability to learn and self-improve makes AI not just a tool but a collaborator in driving innovation.

AI Capabilities and Applications

Given the wealth of potential applications for AI, it's helpful to organize them from the perspective of the AI system's capabilities as well as based on the type of application.

AI's Core Capabilities

AI's capabilities (Figure 4.2) are expanding rapidly. At their core, however, today's systems excel in five major areas:

- **Writing:** AI can be used for writing tasks ranging from generating email drafts to crafting entire articles or ad campaigns. Tools like Jasper and ChatGPT allow businesses to automate and personalize written content.
- **Understanding Visuals:** AI can analyze images and videos, enabling applications like facial recognition, product tagging, and visual inspections in manufacturing.
- **Hearing and Replicating Audio:** AI can transcribe meetings, translate spoken language in real time, and even mimic human voices for customer interactions.
- **Synthesizing Information:** AI can analyze data to make predictions and recommendations, helping businesses forecast sales, optimize supply chains, or identify market trends.
- **Re-creation of Content in Multiple Formats:** AI doesn't just replicate content; it creates it. From generating marketing videos to designing product prototypes, AI tools enable rapid and scalable creativity.

Today's Core Capabilities of AI

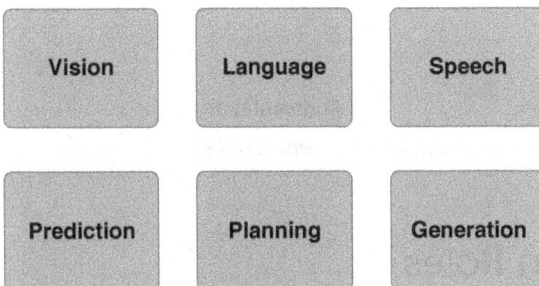

FIGURE 4.2 Core Capabilities of AI

Categories of AI Applications

To navigate AI's limitless potential, it's helpful to categorize its applications (Figure 4.3). There are three application areas in which AI may prove particularly useful:

- **Role-Based Functions:** AI can support individual roles, acting as— for example—a marketing assistant, financial analyst, or customer service representative.

- **Business Functions:** Core business areas like operations, finance, and human resources can benefit from automation and intelligent decision making.

- **Industry-Specific Applications:** Tailored solutions for fields like healthcare, retail, and manufacturing address unique challenges, such as patient diagnostics or inventory forecasting.

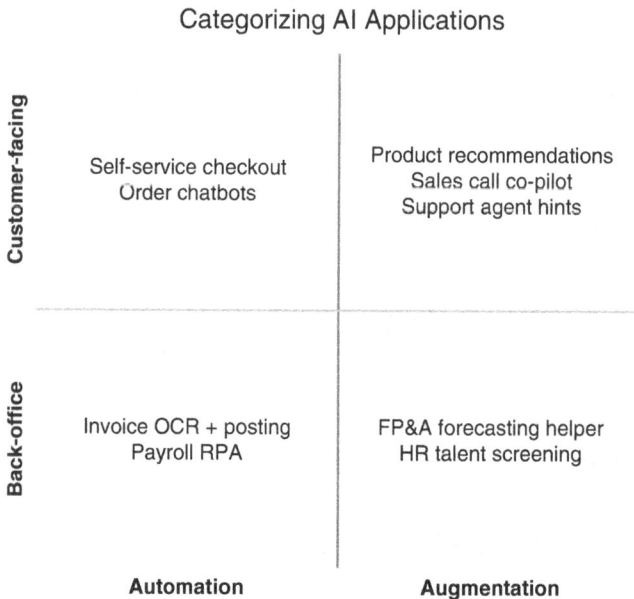

Categorizing AI Applications

	Automation	Augmentation
Customer-facing	Self-service checkout Order chatbots	Product recommendations Sales call co-pilot Support agent hints
Back-office	Invoice OCR + posting Payroll RPA	FP&A forecasting helper HR talent screening

FIGURE 4.3 Framework for Categorizing AI Applications

AI's Impact on Roles

The integration of AI into businesses is reshaping roles at every level of the organizational structure. One of the most profound changes is the flattening of organizational hierarchies.

Traditionally, organizational charts have featured some variant of the same hierarchical structure: a CEO at the top, followed by a cascade of C-suite executives, directors, managers, and individual contributors. However, the rise of AI is challenging this model by enabling individuals to take on responsibilities that were once distributed across multiple layers of the hierarchy.

The Rise of the One-Person Powerhouse

In Silicon Valley, there's a race to create the first one-person billion-dollar company. While this goal might seem ambitious, it's already feasible. During the Internet age, individuals were able to build million-dollar businesses by leveraging online tools. Now, with the productivity gains from AI and agents, one person can manage multiple aspects of a business—marketing, finance, operations, and even customer service.

For example, an entrepreneur could use AI in the following ways:

- **AI for Marketing:** Tools like Jasper or Midjourney to create ad campaigns.
- **AI for Operations:** Workflow automation with Zapier or UiPath.
- **AI for Finance:** Forecasting and budgeting with Copilot in Excel.

Implications for Larger Organizations

While small businesses and startups are often quick to adopt AI, larger enterprises tend to integrate such drastic changes much more slowly. However, as hybrid companies—those that employ a mix of human workers and AI systems—outperform traditional models, legacy businesses will be forced to adapt or risk falling behind.

Transitioning to the Role of the Orchestrator

In this evolving workplace, professionals must embrace a new role: the **Orchestrator**. This involves moving from performing individual tasks to managing a system of AI tools and human collaborators.

For many professionals, this shift presents two key challenges based on their starting point:

- **From Individual Contributor or Manager to Orchestrator**
  - **Strength:** Familiarity with executing tasks and managing details.
  - **Challenge:** Letting go of the minutiae to focus on the bigger picture—that is, creating and directing.

- From C-Suite to Orchestrator
  - **Strength:** Vision and leadership experience.
  - **Challenge:** Gaining hands-on familiarity with AI tools to understand their capabilities and guide their integration effectively.

Practical Steps to Embrace the Orchestrator Role

No matter what your starting point is, developing Orchestrator skills is achievable. Here's how to begin:

Step 1. Build Solo Projects

- Choose a fun or meaningful project. For example, create a blog, develop a marketing campaign, or analyze a dataset with AI tools.
- Use this project as a sandbox to test AI's capabilities and discover how it can complement your skillset.

Step 2. Identify Gaps

- Reflect on areas where you lack experience (e.g., finance, strategy, or graphic design).
- Leverage AI to bridge those gaps and expand your capabilities.

Step 3. Practice Orchestrating

- Experiment with directing multiple AI tools to complete a task.
- For instance, use ChatGPT to draft an email campaign, Canva for visuals, and Zapier to automate distribution.

Example: An Orchestrator in Action

Imagine you're a manager in a retail company looking to boost sales. As an Orchestrator, you might rely on AI in the following ways:

- Use Claude/ChatGPT to analyze past sales data and identify trends.
- Generate personalized marketing materials with Midjourney and Jasper.
- Automate inventory restocking using predictive AI tools.

By orchestrating these tools, you can streamline workflows, reduce costs, and focus your time on innovation.

AI in Marketing

AI is being applied to optimize marketing in myriad ways that touch every aspect of the field—from strategic planning to creative execution and performance analysis.

The Evolution of Marketing

Marketing has already undergone a digital transformation. Before digital tools were available, a key challenge was determining whether a campaign was working, and identifying which elements of the campaign were driving success was just a pipe dream. Digital marketing introduced tracking, testing, and measuring capabilities, requiring marketers to develop **data literacy**.

Even before generative AI entered the realm of possibility, discriminative AI was making waves in marketing:

* **Algorithms Like K-Means Clustering:** Group customers by behaviors or demographics, enabling personalized, targeted campaigns.

* **Recommendation Engines:** Pioneered by companies like Amazon and Target, these systems analyze purchase patterns to suggest complementary products.

Generative AI's Role in Marketing

The advent of generative AI has introduced a new era in **creative marketing**:

* Content Creation at Scale
  * Tools like Jasper and ChatGPT can generate email copy, social media posts, and ad text in seconds, personalized for specific audiences.
  * Visual content creation tools like Midjourney and DALL-E enable designers to create custom graphics or prototypes effortlessly.

* Hyper-Personalization
  * AI's ability to process data at scale allows for personalized visuals, copy, and audio tailored to individual preferences, enhancing engagement.
  * Imagine an ad campaign where every user sees creative elements customized to their demographics, interests, and behaviors.

* Rapid Ideation and Prototyping
  * Marketers can use AI to brainstorm campaign concepts, iterate on designs, and test variations before full-scale rollout.
  * For example, an AI tool might generate 10 variations of a slogan, suggest themes for a video, or design multiple layouts for a website.

Data Analysis for Marketers

Marketing is as much about analysis as it is about creativity. Many teams, however, lack the advanced analytical skills needed to interpret complex campaign data. AI bridges this gap:

- **Simplified Analysis:** Upload spreadsheets into a tool like GPT or Excel Copilot, ask specific questions (e.g., "Which campaign had the highest ROI?"), and receive actionable insights.
- **Market Trends:** Tools like Sprinklr and Hootsuite analyze social media sentiment and trends, enabling marketers to stay ahead of the curve.
- **Predictive Insights:** AI can forecast customer behaviors, helping marketers allocate their budgets more effectively.

Automated A/B Testing

The A/B testing process has long been a cornerstone of performance optimization. Today, it has reached new levels with AI:

- AI tools can autonomously generate, test, and optimize variations of ad copy, visuals, or layouts in real time.
- For instance, Google's AI-driven Performance Max campaigns dynamically adjust creatives based on audience engagement, maximizing effectiveness.

Small Business Marketing Applications

AI's marketing benefits aren't limited to just large corporations. Businesses, which are often constrained by limited budgets and resources, can use AI to step up their marketing efforts:

- **Create Professional Content:** Use Canva's AI-powered features for quick, polished designs.
- **Optimize Social Media:** Leverage tools like Buffer and ChatGPT to craft posts and schedule them efficiently.
- **Analyze Customer Behavior:** Employ affordable platforms like Zoho to gain insights into customer preferences.

AI in Sales

AI is poised to transform sales by streamlining processes, automating repetitive tasks, and enhancing the **human element** of customer relationships. This dual approach—that is, automating what can be automated while elevating personal connections—addresses the growing challenge of cutting through the noise in an increasingly digital world.

Automating Sales Processes

AI tools are already making inroads into sales by automating the following tasks:

- **Lead Gathering:** Platforms like Salesforce and HubSpot use AI agents to collect relevant information about prospects, including their demographics, behaviors, and preferences.

- **Follow-Ups and Reminders:** Intelligent assistants can schedule follow-ups, send reminders, and keep prospects engaged through automated yet personalized communication.

- **Contract Drafting and Negotiation:** AI-powered tools can draft contracts based on templates and even suggest negotiation strategies to expedite deal closures.

For example, a salesperson preparing for a meeting with a high-value prospect can use an AI-powered customer relationship management (CRM) system to instantly retrieve the prospect's interaction history, preferences, and recent inquiries, saving hours of manual research.

Enhancing Prospecting and Presentations

AI doesn't just automate processes; it enhances the strategic aspects of sales:

- **Prospecting:** Predictive analytics tools like Apollo and LinkedIn Sales Navigator can identify potential leads based on buying signals or market trends.

- **Tailored Pitches:** AI can analyze a prospect's business and provide insights, helping sales professionals craft presentations that directly address the prospect's needs and challenges.

- **Customer Understanding:** Sentiment analysis tools evaluate customer interactions, allowing sales teams to gauge satisfaction levels and tailor their approach accordingly.

For example, AI might analyze a prospect's social media activity and provide insights into their current priorities, enabling a salesperson to create a highly relevant pitch.

Fostering Deeper Relationships

In a world flooded with automated cold emails and generic LinkedIn messages, **personal connections** will become the distinguishing factor for successful sales professionals. AI enables this by:

- Taking over routine administrative tasks, freeing salespeople to focus on relationship-building.
- Providing data-driven insights that empower meaningful, personalized interactions.

For instance, instead of sending a generic follow-up, a salesperson can use AI insights to reference a prospect's recent business achievements or tailor messaging to their industry trends.

Business Sales Applications

Businesses can leverage AI to elevate their sales game:

- **AI Email Assistants:** Automate email responses with tools like ChatGPT for Business.
- **Custom CRMs:** Affordable platforms like Zoho can streamline lead management.
- **Automated Call Scheduling:** AI scheduling assistants can reduce back-and-forth communication with clients.

AI in Operations

AI has the potential to transform business operations across a wide spectrum of activities. To clarify its applications in this area, we can categorize them into five key areas: process/project management, supply chain, customer service, quality control, and facilities management.

Process and Project Management

AI tools are streamlining how teams plan, execute, and monitor their workflows:

- **Automation of Routine Tasks:** Tools like Zapier and UiPath automate repetitive workflows, reducing human intervention and minimizing errors.
- **Custom GPTs:** Teams can now deploy GPT-based assistants to create timelines, generate flowcharts, highlight bottlenecks, and send automated reminders.

- **Predictive Project Analysis:** AI-powered tools can analyze past project data to predict potential delays and recommend adjustments.

For example, a marketing agency can use AI to automate the creation of weekly task updates, integrating the AI capabilities with tools like Asana or Trello for seamless project tracking.

Customer Service

Customer service is one of the fastest-growing areas for AI adoption, with **large language models (LLMs)** leading the charge:

- **Chat-Based Support:** AI-driven chatbots like Zendesk AI provide immediate, accurate responses, ensuring 24/7 support.
- **Voice Call Automation:** Thanks to advancements in natural language processing and audio re-creation, AI now powers human-sounding voice assistants.
- **Proactive Assistance:** AI can predict customer needs based on interaction history, offering solutions before an issue arises.

As one example, Klarya saved millions by implementing AI-powered voice call systems that handle common customer inquiries. The systems escalate only complex cases to human agents.

Supply Chain Management

AI applications in supply chain operations have existed for years, but **digital twins** are now pushing their boundaries ahead:

- **Simulation and Forecasting:** AI-driven models can simulate supply chain workflows, predicting disruptions and optimizing resource allocation.
- **Digital Twins:** These virtual replicas of physical spaces, whether a factory floor or an entire city, help businesses test scenarios and plan strategically.
- **AI in Robotics:** Companies like Amazon already use robots for order fulfillment. Innovators like Tesla and Figure AI are now developing humanoid robots to carry out complex tasks such as food preparation and assembly.

For example, one manufacturing plant uses digital twins to optimize its production schedules and preempt equipment failures.

Quality Control

AI excels in detecting anomalies and ensuring high-quality standards:

- **Automated Inspections:** Machine vision systems can analyze products for defects at scales and speeds unattainable by human inspectors.
- **Predictive Maintenance:** AI can predict when equipment is likely to fail, reducing downtime and saving costs.

As an example, a food packaging company uses AI to inspect thousands of items per hour, ensuring compliance with safety standards.

Facilities Management

Managing physical spaces becomes significantly easier with AI assistance:

- **Energy Optimization:** AI-powered systems can regulate HVAC, lighting, and energy consumption based on real-time usage data.
- **Smart Maintenance:** Sensors connected to AI systems can monitor facilities and trigger alerts for repairs or maintenance.

For example, a commercial office building uses AI to optimize its energy consumption. This system has reduced the building's costs by 30% annually.

AI in Finance

Finance professionals have always relied on tools like spreadsheets to organize and analyze data, and AI is becoming the ultimate partner for this work. Whether it's enhancing efficiency, generating precise forecasts, or helping with decision making, AI is adding a layer of intelligence to financial processes that makes day-to-day tasks go more smoothly. These advancements are especially useful for time-consuming tasks such as transaction classification or building financial models, allowing analysts and accountants to focus more on strategy and insights instead of repetitive manual work.

AI-Powered Tools for Financial Analysis

The marriage of AI and spreadsheets opens up new possibilities:

- **Plugins and Assistants:** Tools like Microsoft's Copilot and GPT-based assistants in Excel or Google Sheets can analyze data, create financial models, and generate visualizations with ease.

- **Forecasting:** AI can analyze historical data, market trends, and macroeconomic indicators to produce accurate financial forecasts.
- **Scenario Planning:** Teams can use AI to simulate various financial scenarios, helping them plan for best- and worst-case outcomes.

For example, a finance team can use an AI tool to predict cash flow for the next quarter, with the AI system adjusting this forecast based on changing market conditions.

Automation in Accounting and Tax Advice

AI is transforming how accountants and tax professionals work:

- **Transaction Classification Tools:** Automatically classify and categorize expenses, streamlining bookkeeping and reducing errors.
- **Tax Advice:** Companies like TurboTax leverage AI for personalized tax guidance, ensuring compliance and uncovering deductions.
- **Audit Automation:** AI tools can perform preliminary audits, flagging discrepancies or anomalies for human review.

For example, a small business accountant can use AI to classify thousands of transactions in minutes, saving hours of manual work.

Challenges: Data Privacy and Security

There are two primary barriers to broader adoption of AI in finance:

- **Data Privacy:** Sensitive financial information must remain secure, especially in highly regulated industries.
- **Integration:** Legacy systems in finance often require significant effort to integrate them with AI solutions.

Emerging Trends

Emerging trends in AI in finance include the following:

- **Embedded AI in Financial Software:** Expect AI capabilities to be integrated directly into popular accounting tools like QuickBooks, enabling real-time analytics and automated reporting.
- **Fraud Detection:** AI systems like SAS Fraud Management can identify unusual patterns in transactions to prevent fraud.
- **Investment Analysis:** Platforms like Bloomberg GPT can analyze market data, providing actionable insights for investment decisions.

AI in Product Development

AI is transforming how products are researched, designed, and brought to market. In this context, AI is no longer limited to just automating tedious tasks; instead, it can be applied to amplify creativity, streamline prototyping, and accelerate time-to-market.

The Research and Discovery Phase

In the research and discovery stage of product development, AI excels at gathering insights, brainstorming ideas, and exploring potential markets:

- **Role-Playing and User Feedback:** LLMs can simulate conversations with target users, offering feedback that helps refine product concepts.
- **Market Research:** Tools like Perplexity.ai can provide sourced insights, helping teams analyze trends and identify gaps in the market without succumbing to misinformation or hallucinations.

For example, a startup exploring a fitness app might use AI to simulate user preferences, gaining insights into features like workout tracking or social connectivity.

Streamlined Prototyping

Prototyping has always been a resource-intensive endeavor, requiring specialized tools and expertise. AI is now changing the game:

- **Generative Design:** Platforms like DALL-E, Midjourney, and Sora allow creators to generate design mockups without prior graphic design skills.
- **Motion Graphics and Animation:** AI tools enable rapid prototyping of dynamic product visuals, saving time and resources.

Here's a real-world application in this area: When developing my immersive art exhibit, I relied on DALL-E and Midjourney to create vivid prototypes. This bypassed the traditional need for hiring external designers and sped up the process, allowing me to focus on refining the concept.

Testing and Refinement

AI's benefits in product development don't stop at creation. These tools can also be applied to enhance testing and iteration:

• **Simulated User Testing:** AI can mimic user interactions to identify usability issues before real-world deployment of the product.

• **A/B Testing:** AI tools can automatically generate and analyze different product variations to identify which resonate most strongly with the intended audience.

For example, a company producing wearable tech might use AI to test multiple interface designs, optimizing the final result for usability and visual appeal.

Small Business and Enterprise Use Cases

• **Small Businesses:** AI tools democratize product development. A solopreneur can ideate, prototype, and test concepts with AI-powered solutions that were once reserved for large companies.

• **Enterprises:** AI accelerates innovation cycles by automating repetitive aspects of product testing and allowing R&D teams to focus on strategic decision making.

Finding the Right AI Applications

Selecting the right AI applications for your business or personal use requires a mix of self-assessment, exploration, and experimentation (Figure 4.4). Here's a simple framework to guide you:

• **Assess Your Needs:** Start by identifying pain points or repetitive tasks in your workflows. Consider:

  • **Time-Intensive Tasks:** Which processes take up most of your time?

  • **Bottlenecks:** Are there areas where tasks get delayed or pile up?

  • **Skill Gaps:** Where do you lack expertise or efficiency?

  Example: If data analysis takes up a lot of your time, look for tools like GPT-based analytics assistants.

• **Explore Existing Tools:** Research tools that are tailored to your industry or specific needs. Consider these approaches:

  • **AI Marketplaces:** Investigate platforms like OpenAI's ChatGPT Plugin Store or Microsoft's AI tools.

- **Competitor Analysis:** Which tools are industry leaders using?
- **Social Media and Blogs:** Follow experts in your field who share practical AI use cases.

Example: If you work in customer service, explore AI chatbots like Zendesk AI and LivePerson.

- **Experiment and Iterate:** Start small by testing one AI tool in a low-risk area of your workflow. Evaluate its performance, and then iterate or scale based on results.

Example: A marketer might use an AI writing assistant like Jasper for creating email copy before expanding its use to other areas of content creation.

How to Find AI Applications: Decision Flow & Iteration Loop

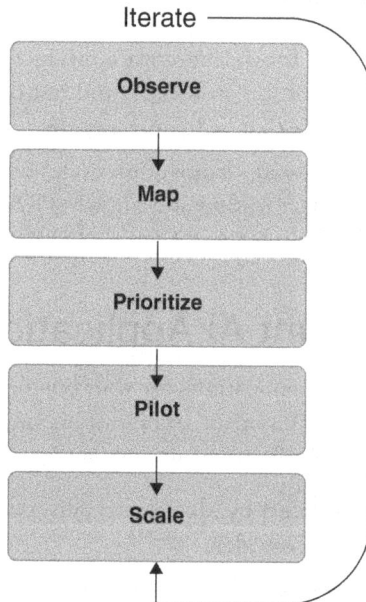

FIGURE 4.4 How to Find AI Applications: Decision Flow and Iteration Loop

Exercise: Identifying AI Applications

Objective: Pinpoint specific AI tools to improve your workflow.

Step 1. Map Your Workflow (15 minutes)

- Write down your daily or weekly tasks.
- Mark tasks that are repetitive, time-consuming, or skill-intensive.

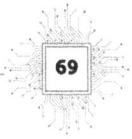

Step 2. Categorize Needs (10 minutes)

- Place tasks into categories: creative, analytical, or both.
- Identify whether these tasks involve text, data, audio, visuals, or strategy.

Step 3. Research AI Tools (20 minutes)

- Use online AI marketplaces or forums to find tools that align with your needs.
- Take note of free trials or low-cost versions you can test.

Step 4. Test and Reflect (1 week)

- Use the tool for one specific task.
- Reflect on the results: Did the tool save time? Improve quality?
- Highlight areas for improvement.

Step 5. Document Your Findings

- Keep a record of your experiments to inform future decisions.

Conclusion

This chapter has explored how AI is transforming businesses across various domains, including marketing, sales, operations, finance, and product development. Whether it's automating repetitive tasks, enhancing creativity, or enabling smarter decision making, AI has proved to be a versatile tool for innovation and growth.

Key Takeaways

Key takeaways include the following:

- From creating personalized marketing campaigns to optimizing supply chains and designing prototypes, AI can address challenges across a wide variety of industries.
- Businesses can start small, testing AI tools in specific areas before scaling their implementation.
- With AI handling routine tasks, professionals can shift their focus to more strategic and creative endeavors.
- Identifying the right AI applications involves trying out tools, iterating, and reflecting on what works best.

Reminders for Implementation

- Assess your specific needs and workflows to identify where AI can add value.

- Start with accessible tools and gradually explore more advanced applications.

- Balance automation with human oversight to ensure accuracy and ethical use.

The potential of AI is immense, but its true power depends on how effectively it's orchestrated within a business. The next chapter dives into the challenges of scaling AI across organizations, building seamless integrations, and unlocking even greater value through collaboration between human and artificial intelligence.

5

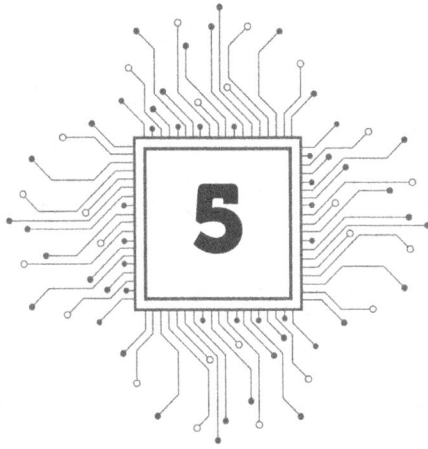

AI Orchestration at Scale

At this point, you should have a basic understanding of how machines can mimic human intelligence, and in some instances, as with Google's AlphaFold, exhibit superhuman intelligence. The next challenge is to fully harness this capability at scale.

AI is no longer a novelty; it's a necessity for individuals and organizations that want to get—and stay—ahead in a rapidly changing world. To leverage AI effectively, we must move beyond simple adoption and into orchestration: the deliberate and strategic integration of AI into every aspect of our work.

The Role of the AI Orchestrator

To become an AI Orchestrator, you need to reimagine how you approach intelligence, creativity, and workflows. This involves embracing AI not just as a tool to complete tasks for you, but also as a partner that can amplify your own abilities.

This requires three foundational steps:

- **Enhancing Your Own Intelligence:** Expanding your capacity to process and apply information by leveraging AI's ability to analyze, summarize, and predict.
- **Optimizing Your Workflows:** Streamlining repetitive or manual tasks with AI, creating systems that work faster and smarter.
- **Creating Without Limits:** Using AI's generative capabilities to explore ideas, develop solutions, and build prototypes at a scale never experienced before.

While the future may bring AI assistants that anticipate our needs and act as true collaborators, we're not there yet. Today, many of the interactions still rely on humans prompting, guiding, and iterating with these systems. This is where orchestration begins.

The Challenge of Knowing What to Ask

Engaging with AI often starts with a question or command: "Generate this report," "Draft a marketing email," or "Summarize this data." While this approach may be effective, it leads to a critical question: *What happens when we don't know what to ask?*

The truth is, many of us aren't used to identifying where we need help, let alone articulating it clearly. For example, a manager might struggle to define how AI could improve team productivity, a designer might not realize that AI could assist with ideation or prototyping, and a marketer might know they want to personalize customer experiences but be unsure where AI fits into that goal.

This uncertainty can lead to missed opportunities, underutilization, and frustration.

Reframing the Fear of Asking for Help

For some people, asking for help, whether from a machine or a person, is a daunting prospect. I'll admit this has always been a challenge for me. It's not because I've had bad experiences with rejection, but because I often don't know where to start. There's a vulnerability in admitting, *I don't know what I need help with.*

AI removes much of the anxiety tied to this fear. Unlike human interactions, AI interactions are free of judgment. If you ask a poorly framed question or get an unhelpful response, the stakes are low. You can simply refine your question and try again.

This iterative process encourages experimentation and reframes failure as part of learning. For example, an initial prompt, such as "How can I improve my social media strategy?", might yield a general response. Refining it to "Can you analyze this data and suggest the best times to post on social media?" could generate actionable insights.

Each interaction teaches you more about the tool's capabilities, and your own ability to communicate effectively.

Understanding the Barriers to AI Integration

The biggest barrier to adopting AI at scale isn't technological—it's psychological. Many individuals struggle to understand where and how AI can integrate into their workstreams to:

- **Enhance Their Intelligence:** Using AI to synthesize information, generate insights, or make decisions with confidence.
- **Automate Routine Tasks:** Reducing time spent on repetitive work such as data entry or scheduling.
- **Boost Creativity:** Partnering with AI tools to brainstorm, iterate, and refine ideas.

To overcome these barriers, we must adopt a mindset of curiosity and exploration. AI orchestration isn't about knowing all the answers, but rather about being willing to ask questions, test ideas, and learn through experimentation.

Practical Example: Bridging the Gap

Imagine you're a project manager overseeing multiple teams. You suspect AI could improve workflows, but you aren't sure where to start. A simple exercise might look like this:

- **Identify a Repetitive Task:** Team members manually input project updates into a spreadsheet.
- **Explore AI Capabilities:** Research automation tools that integrate with project management platforms, such as Asana and Monday.com.
- **Test and Iterate:** Deploy a small automation to extract updates from Slack messages and populate the spreadsheet automatically.
- **Reflect and Scale:** Evaluate the time saved and expand the use of AI into other areas, such as generating progress reports or forecasting deadlines.

This process shown in Figure 5.1 illustrates how AI can support both immediate needs and long-term goals, turning uncertainty into action.

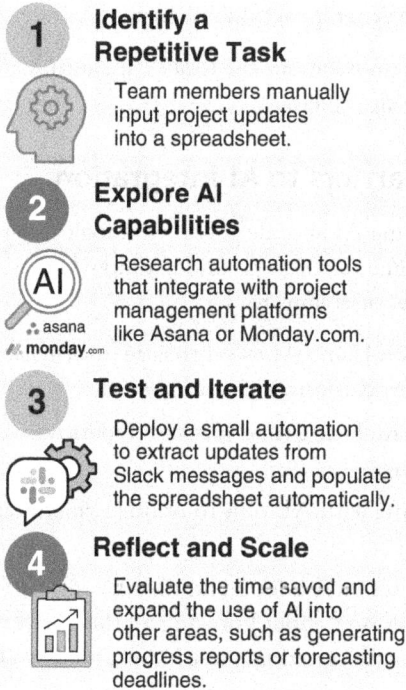

1 Identify a Repetitive Task

Team members manually input project updates into a spreadsheet.

2 Explore AI Capabilities

Research automation tools that integrate with project management platforms like Asana or Monday.com.

asana
monday.com

3 Test and Iterate

Deploy a small automation to extract updates from Slack messages and populate the spreadsheet automatically.

4 Reflect and Scale

Evaluate the time saved and expand the use of AI into other areas, such as generating progress reports or forecasting deadlines.

FIGURE 5.1 Method for AI Adoption

Shifting the Paradigm

Becoming an AI Orchestrator isn't about mastering every tool—it's about mastering the mindset. It's about asking, *How can this make me better, faster, or more creative?* When you adopt this perspective, the barriers to adoption fade, and the possibilities for integration become limitless.

Becoming the Observer

In 2014, I bought a planner that divided each day into 30-minute increments. At first, I tried to meticulously plan my days, blocking off appointments, scheduling focus time, and even penciling in workouts. But life didn't cooperate: Meetings ran late, interruptions were constant, and despite my best intentions, I often skipped my workout because I was too tired. Instead of feeling productive, I felt defeated.

What was supposed to help me achieve more ended up making me feel worse. So, I pivoted.

Turning Planning into Observation

Instead of writing what I *planned* to do, I began filling in what I had actually done the day before. Suddenly, my planner became a treasure trove of accurate data. After just a few weeks, I noticed something powerful: By reflecting on my patterns and behaviors, I could make small adjustments that improved my days.

For example, I realized I was wasting more time than I thought scrolling through social media or watching TV. I discovered pockets of available time I didn't know I had.

These small insights added up. Thirty minutes a day may not feel like much, but over a week, or a year, it becomes significant.

Fast forward ten years, and I'm still tracking my time. I've optimized the process and even designed my own planner. (Fun fact: Ask me what I was doing on any day in the past decade, and I can tell you. It's a great party trick!)

But beyond the novelty, this practice highlights an important point: Most people don't remember what they did two days ago. While our lives are full of tools designed to make things easier, we're busier than ever, running from one meeting to the next, drowning in emails, and just trying to stay afloat.

Where AI Comes In

I understand why people feel skeptical when they hear that AI will make their lives easier. "How?" they ask. "I'm already overwhelmed. Where will I find the time to learn new tools or update my workflows?"

Here's the secret: You don't need to overhaul everything at once. Instead, by observing your patterns and reflecting on how you spend your time, you can find targeted areas where AI can provide immediate help. Small changes can then lead to big transformations.

Exercise: Understanding Your Patterns

This exercise is designed to help you identify where your time goes and where AI could make the biggest difference. It takes just 10 minutes a day for two weeks, but the insights you'll gain will be invaluable.

Week 1: Tracking Your Time

Step 1. Record what you do in 30-minute increments each day.

- Use Excel, Google Sheets, or paper (download a free template at The Observer Store).
- The best time to fill out the tracker is at the end of each day, but the next morning works, too. Avoid waiting longer than 48 hours to ensure accuracy.
- Be honest! If you spent 30 minutes scrolling LinkedIn or zoning out, write it down.

Step 2. Reflect at the end of the week. Ask yourself:

- What patterns did you notice?
- Were you surprised by how you spent your time?
- Are there areas where your time use doesn't align with your goals or values?

Week 2: Integrating AI into Your Workflow

Step 1. Highlight tasks from Week 1 that AI could assist with. Here are some examples:

- Managing emails
- Creating social media posts
- Drafting memos or reports
- Brainstorming strategies or generating ideas

Step 2. Prioritize those tasks.

- Which one would provide the greatest relief or impact if automated or assisted by AI? Start there.

Step 3. Carve out 30 minutes this week to experiment with AI for your chosen task.

- For example: Use ChatGPT to summarize emails or Jasper to write a blog draft.

Tips for Success

1. Write your goal for Week 2 at the top of your tracker (e.g., "Experiment with AI for creating email responses").
2. Keep tracking your time to hold yourself accountable.
3. Reflect at the end of the week:

   - Did you meet your goal?
   - Did AI make a difference in your workflow?

Why This Matters

This exercise isn't just about productivity; it's also about recognizing that you *do* have time. By understanding your workflow and starting small, you'll see how AI can free you from routine tasks and enable you to focus on what matters most.

Whether you continue tracking your time after two weeks or not, the key takeaways from this exercise are as follows:

- **Awareness:** Knowing how you spend your time is the first step toward making meaningful changes.
- **Opportunity:** Once you see where AI fits in, you can start using it to lighten your workload.
- **Action:** Start with small, manageable changes and build from there.

Remember: The goal isn't perfection, it's progress. The more intentional you are about how you spend your time, the more effectively you'll be able to orchestrate your life and work, with AI as your ally.

Personal AI Orchestration at Scale

After completing the two-week exercise in understanding your time and integrating AI into your workflow, your journey toward personal AI orchestration truly begins. The key to success is consistency and gradual exploration. It's not about overwhelming yourself with tools or trends; instead, it's about building sustainable habits that let AI enhance your capabilities over time.

Start Small and Build Gradually

One of the biggest mistakes people make when incorporating AI into their workflow is trying to do too much, too fast. It's tempting to dive into the world of AI headfirst, experimenting with every tool and trying to overhaul your entire workflow in one fell swoop. But this often leads to frustration, burnout, and ultimately abandoning the effort.

My advice: Start with *one task* and *one tool*. For example, if managing your emails feels overwhelming, begin with a tool like ChatGPT that can help you draft responses or summarize threads. If brainstorming content ideas is a challenge, experiment with Jasper or Perplexity.ai to generate concepts.

Focus on mastering one tool to improve one part of your workflow before expanding further.

Ignore the Noise

In the AI space, it's easy to feel distracted by the tech bros who list ten models they "brilliantly" use for specific tasks, all while touting their superhuman productivity. This noise can create unnecessary pressure to adopt the latest and greatest tools, but here's the truth: *AI is evolving rapidly.* Most tools release updates every 4–8 months, meaning today's "best" model will soon be matched or surpassed by its competitors. *What matters most is value.* Are you getting tangible benefits from the tool you're using? If so, stick with it instead of chasing trends.

It's better to extract meaningful value from a single tool than to spread yourself thin across multiple platforms without a clear purpose.

Stay Curious and Seek Inspiration

Even with a focused approach, it's essential to stay inspired. AI's capabilities are constantly evolving, and new use cases emerge every day. Here's how to keep your ideas fresh:

1. **Look for Inspiration**
   - Follow industry leaders or creators who share practical examples of how they're using AI.
   - Join communities or forums where people exchange ideas and tips.

2. **Experiment Weekly**
   - Push yourself to test at least one new feature or use case every week. For example:
     - Try using Midjourney to create visuals for a presentation.
     - Use AI to automate scheduling with tools like Motion or Reclaim.
     - Experiment with AI transcription tools like Otter.ai to summarize meetings.
   - What's the cost? Likely no more than 30 minutes—time that you now know how to repurpose from the earlier exercise.

3. **Evaluate Periodically**
   - Every six months, reassess your AI toolkit. Ask yourself:
     - Am I still getting significant value from the tools I'm using?
     - Have new models emerged that could improve my workflow?
   - This periodic review ensures you stay up-to-date without chasing every shiny new tool that hits the market.

Examples of Personal AI Orchestration

Here's how a deliberate, step-by-step approach to AI orchestration might look in practice:

- Month 1
  - **Task:** Automate meeting note summaries.
  - **Tool:** Implement Otter.ai to transcribe and summarize your meetings.
  - **Goal:** Free up time spent manually writing summaries.
- Month 2
  - **Task:** Improve content creation for emails or blogs.
  - **Tool:** Use Jasper to generate drafts based on your ideas.
  - **Goal:** Spend less time writing from scratch while maintaining a consistent voice.
- Month 3
  - **Task:** Optimize calendar management.
  - **Tool:** Integrate Reclaim.ai to schedule tasks automatically and reduce the amount of time spent juggling priorities.
  - **Goal:** Increase focus time and reduce scheduling conflicts.

Over time, these incremental improvements will add up, transforming your workflow without overwhelming you.

The Balance Between Focus and Exploration

Although I don't recommend adopting four or five tools simultaneously, exploring new possibilities is essential. The trick is finding a balance: Use your primary tools to handle your core tasks consistently. Experiment weekly with small, manageable features or use cases to expand your understanding of AI's potential.

By sticking to this approach, you'll avoid stagnation while ensuring you don't lose sight of your overall goals.

Key Takeaways for Personal AI Orchestration

When striving for personal orchestration as a means to improve your workflow, here are key points:

- **Start Small:** Focus on one task and one tool at a time to build confidence and avoid burnout.

- **Stay Focused:** Prioritize extracting meaningful value from your current tools rather than chasing trends.

- **Push Boundaries:** Regularly experiment with new features or use cases to discover fresh opportunities.

- **Reflect and Adjust:** Every six months, evaluate your tools to ensure they align with your evolving needs.

By staying consistent and curious, you'll become not just an AI user but also an Orchestrator. That is, you'll be able to seamlessly integrate AI into your work to unlock new levels of productivity and creativity.

Task Automation

So far, we've explored how generative AI can enhance productivity and creativity. But AI's capabilities extend beyond ideation and assistance, into the realm of **task automation**. This is where **robotic process automation (RPA)** comes into play. While less glamorous than generative AI, RPA is a powerful tool for streamlining repetitive tasks, improving efficiency, and freeing up your mental bandwidth.

What Is RPA?

RPA uses software robots, or "bots," to perform repetitive, rule-based tasks that humans typically handle. These tasks often involve the following skills:

- **Data Entry:** Transferring information between systems or copying and pasting data.

- **Transaction Processing:** Approving invoices, processing orders, or handling payroll.

- **Report Generation:** Compiling and formatting information into spreadsheets or dashboards.

Unlike generative AI, RPA does not "think" or "learn"; instead, it follows a strict set of procedural commands. For example, an RPA bot might log into an email account, download attachments, and upload them into a database, all without human intervention.

The benefits of RPA are clear:

- **Speed:** Bots can work faster than humans.

- **Accuracy:** Bots can eliminate errors caused by fatigue or oversight.

- **Cost Savings:** Automating time-consuming tasks can reduce labor costs.
- **Focus:** Employees can spend more time on creative, strategic, or value-driven work.

How to Identify Tasks for Automation

One challenge when pursuing RPA is pinpointing the right tasks to automate. Often, these tasks feel insignificant in isolation, and they may take only a few seconds or minutes to complete. Over time, though, their repetitive nature adds up.

Here's a simple way to identify automation opportunities:

- **Look for Repetition:** Tasks performed daily or weekly, such as downloading reports or sending invoices, are good candidates.
- **Follow the Rules:** Processes with clear, consistent rules are perfect for bots. For example, "If X happens, do Y."
- **Time and Frustration:** Tasks that eat into your day or feel like a drain on your energy are strong candidates.

Figure 5.2 depicts these concepts visually.

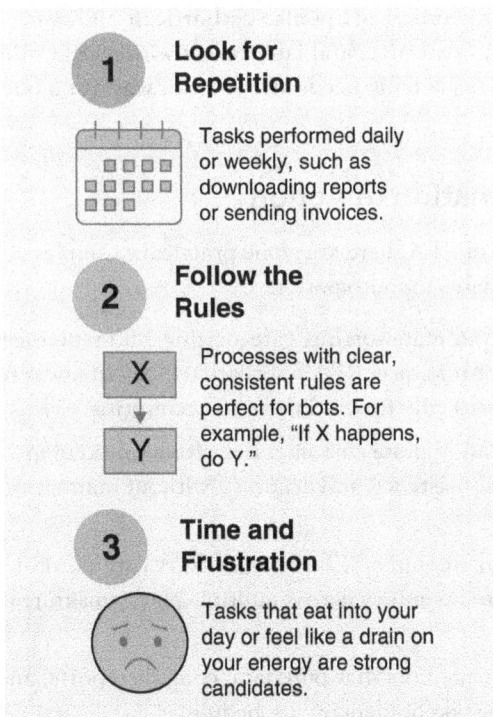

1 Look for Repetition
Tasks performed daily or weekly, such as downloading reports or sending invoices.

2 Follow the Rules
Processes with clear, consistent rules are perfect for bots. For example, "If X happens, do Y."

3 Time and Frustration
Tasks that eat into your day or feel like a drain on your energy are strong candidates.

FIGURE 5.2 How to Identify Tasks for Automation

The Power of Reflection: My Offboarding List

I keep a running note on my phone titled "Offboard." Anytime I encounter a task that feels:

- Like it's a waste of my time,
- Delegable to someone else, or
- Just plain annoying,

I add it to this list.

Every few months, I review this list and sort the tasks into three categories:

- **Offboard to Someone Else:** If a task doesn't require my expertise, I delegate it to a team member or hire someone to handle it. For example, social media scheduling or customer follow-ups might fall into this category.
- **Stop Doing:** Some tasks lose their relevance over time. Reviewing the list helps identify outdated practices that no longer serve my goals.
- **Automate:** Tasks with repetitive, rule-based processes are flagged for automation, saving time and reducing errors.

Keeping this list is not only practical but also cathartic. It allows me to capture my frustrations in real time, and later reflect with a clear mind to determine whether the task truly needs attention or was just a one-off annoyance.

Examples of Automation in Action

To inspire your own use of RPA, here are some practical examples you might consider as candidates for automation:

- **Email Management:** Automate sorting, categorizing, and replying to standard inquiries. For instance, RPA bots can identify invoices in your inbox and automatically forward them to accounting.
- **Data Transfers:** Bots can migrate customer data from one system to another, ensuring consistency and accuracy without manual intervention.
- **Inventory Updates:** For e-commerce businesses, RPA can monitor stock levels and update inventory across multiple platforms in real time.
- **Recurring Reports:** Create bots that pull data, compile reports, and email those reports to stakeholders on a schedule.

• **Scheduling:** RPA tools like Reclaim.ai can automatically schedule meetings, allocate focus time, and optimize your calendar.

The Intersection of RPA and Generative AI

While RPA focuses on repetitive tasks, generative AI can complement these efforts by handling creative or strategic elements. For example:

• **RPA + AI for Customer Support:** RPA bots can handle routine data entry while generative AI chatbots engage with customers in real time.

• **RPA + AI for Reporting:** Bots can collect data and feed it to generative AI tools, which then produce narrative-style reports or executive summaries.

This synergy allows businesses and individuals to achieve a seamless flow between routine automation and higher-order thinking.

Getting Started with Task Automation

Here's a simple process to identify and implement automation:

• **Track Your Work:** Complete the tracking exercise described earlier in this chapter to identify repetitive tasks in your workflow.

• **Categorize Tasks:** Sort tasks into the three buckets: delegate, stop, and automate.

• **Explore Tools:** Research RPA tools like UiPath, Zapier, or Blue Prism to find the best fit for your needs.

• **Start Small:** Begin by automating one simple process, then expand as you grow more confident.

Why Task Automation Matters

Task automation does more than just save time: It frees you to focus on what truly matters. When you offload your repetitive work to bots, you can dedicate more energy to strategic thinking, creative exploration, and making human connections.

With the right approach, automation becomes a powerful enabler, turning mundane tasks into opportunities for growth and innovation.

AI Agents

AI agents represent the next frontier in automation, bridging the gap between static processes (RPA) and dynamic intelligence. As these systems evolve, they will become indispensable for tasks requiring adaptability, decision making, and real-time responsiveness. By understanding the strengths and limitations of AI agents, organizations can strategically integrate them to drive innovation and efficiency across a wide variety of domains.

How AI Agents Differ from RPA

While RPA focuses on automating repetitive, rule-based tasks, AI agents take automation to the next level by introducing autonomy, adaptability, and intelligence. Both RPA and AI agents aim to enhance efficiency and free up human resources for higher-value activities, but the two technologies differ in critical ways.

RPA bots are limited to following predefined rules and executing specific commands in a static manner. For instance, an RPA bot might log into a system, download a report, and email it to a designated recipient. While efficient, the bot cannot adjust its behavior if the workflow changes or errors arise.

AI agents, in contrast, are *dynamic* and *adaptive* (Figure 5.3). These intelligent systems can do the following:

- Perceive their environment
- Make decisions based on past interactions or new data
- Take autonomous actions to achieve a goal

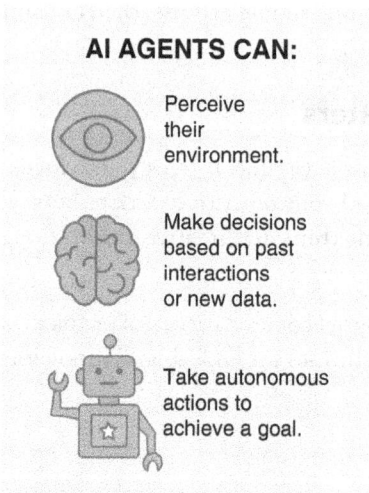

AI AGENTS CAN:

Perceive their environment.

Make decisions based on past interactions or new data.

Take autonomous actions to achieve a goal.

FIGURE 5.3 Core Components of AI Agents

Unlike RPA, AI agents can learn from their experiences, plan future actions, and adjust their approach in real time, making them far more versatile in complex scenarios.

How AI Agents Differ from Generative AI

It's also important to distinguish AI agents from generative AI. Generative AI focuses on creating content, such as text, images, or videos, based on user prompts. AI agents, by contrast, focus on decision making and action, often combining multiple capabilities (including generative AI) to achieve broader objectives.

Here's an example: An AI agent might use generative AI to draft an email. However, it might also query a customer relationship management (CRM) system for relevant customer details and decide when to send the email based on engagement data.

The Core Capabilities of AI Agents

At their heart, AI agents are sophisticated entities designed to perceive their environment, make decisions, and take action. What truly sets them apart are a handful of key characteristics that enable them to operate with a remarkable degree of intelligence and autonomy.

One of their most crucial capabilities is **planning**. An AI agent doesn't just react; it strategizes. It can construct a detailed, step-by-step plan to reach a specific objective, complete with intermediate goals and milestones. Imagine a logistics agent tasked with optimizing a delivery fleet. It wouldn't just send drivers out randomly. Instead, it would analyze all destinations, traffic patterns, and delivery windows to create the most efficient multi-stop routes, continuously reevaluating and adjusting the plan in real time as new orders or unexpected road closures pop up.

This planning is supported by a robust **memory**. Agents combine short-term memory, for tracking information in the immediate present, with long-term memory, which stores knowledge from every past interaction. Think of an AI-powered personal shopping assistant. Its short-term memory holds the details of your current search: "Blue running shoes, size 10." Meanwhile, its long-term memory recalls your past purchases, brand preferences, and even items you've previously browsed but didn't buy. This allows the shopping assistant to offer highly personalized recommendations: "I see you bought a pair of Swiftwick socks last month. Would you like to add another pair to go with your new shoes?"

Agents also excel at **tool usage**. They are not confined to their own internal knowledge, but can also interact with the digital world in powerful ways. An agent can be programmed to access a company's internal database, query a third-party API for fresh data, or even execute a piece of code to perform a complex calculation. For example, a financial analysis agent might be asked to assess the health of a company. It could autonomously pull the latest stock prices via a financial API, access the company's quarterly reports from a database, run a sentiment analysis on recent news articles, and then synthesize all that information into a concise, actionable report.

Underpinning all of these capabilities is **perception**—the ability to gather and interpret information from the surrounding environment. This "environment" could be digital, such as a stream of data from the Internet, or physical, accessed via sensors. In a smart factory, an AI agent might use computer vision to "see" a production line, identifying microscopic defects in a product that the human eye would miss. Simultaneously, it might process data from temperature and vibration sensors to predict when a machine will need maintenance, preventing costly breakdowns before they happen.

Finally, these capabilities culminate in **autonomy.** An AI agent can make independent decisions and adapt its behavior without constant human oversight. Consider an autonomous AI assistant managing a busy executive's calendar. If an urgent, high-priority meeting request comes in, the agent doesn't just flag it. It analyzes the executive's schedule, identifies a lower-priority meeting that can be moved, checks the calendars of all other attendees to find a new slot, and then reschedules it, all without any direct command. The AI tool has the authority and intelligence to manage complex scheduling conflicts on its own.

Types of AI Agents

While all AI agents share these core traits, they can be categorized based on their level of intelligence and the mechanisms that drive their decisions.

The most basic are **simple reflex agents**. These agents operate on a straightforward "if-then" logic, responding directly to their immediate sensory input without considering the history or future consequences. A smart home thermostat is a classic example. If it senses the room temperature has dropped below 68°F, its rule is to turn on the heat. It doesn't remember that you always turn the heat down at night or that a window is open; it simply reacts to the present moment.

A step up are **model-based reflex agents**. These agents maintain an internal "model" or representation of their environment. This allows them to handle situations where they can't see everything at once. For instance, a self-driving car's AI needs to know more than just what its cameras see. It maintains a model of the world around it—for example, tracking a car that has just moved into its blind spot. This internal state allows the AI to "remember" the other car's presence and predict its likely position, enabling the driver to safely change lanes.

Goal-based agents are even more sophisticated. They don't just react or maintain a model; they actively work toward a specific goal. This requires the agents to consider the future outcomes of their actions. Your GPS or navigation app is a good example of a goal-based agent. Your goal is to get to a specific address. The agent has access to multiple paths and evaluates each one based on factors such as distance, current traffic, and road closures. It also simulates the different routes to determine which one will best achieve the goal of arriving at your destination in the shortest amount of time.

Taking this a level further, **utility-based agents** aim to maximize the "utility" or overall happiness of the proposed solution. This is crucial when there are conflicting goals or when some outcomes are better than others. An automated investment agent is a prime example. Its goal isn't just to "make money," but rather to balance aggressive growth with risk tolerance. This AI agent might choose a slightly less profitable investment if it is significantly safer, thereby maximizing the overall utility for a risk-averse client.

Finally, **learning agents** are the most advanced AI agents. They are designed to improve their own performance over time by learning from their experiences. These agents have a "learning element" that analyzes their successes and failures and modifies their decision-making processes accordingly. A spam filter is a simple learning agent. Every time you mark an email as "spam" or "not spam," you are providing feedback to its learning element. It analyzes the features of those emails, including the sender, the keywords, and the links, and refines its algorithm to become more accurate at filtering your inbox in the future.

Real-World Applications of AI Agents

The practical applications of these intelligent agents are already transforming entire industries.

In customer service, AI agents are becoming the first point of contact for many businesses. Companies like Salesforce use AI-powered Einstein Bots to handle a wide range of customer interactions. These agents can answer frequently asked questions, guide a user through a troubleshooting process, or process a return request. They can also access the customer's order history to provide personalized support. If the issue becomes too complex, they can seamlessly gather all relevant information before escalating the conversation to a human agent, ensuring a smooth handoff.

Healthcare is another area seeing massive benefits from this technology. AI agents can analyze medical images like X-rays or magnetic resonance images (MRIs), often detecting signs of disease with a level of accuracy that matches or even exceeds that of human radiologists. They can also function as diagnostic assistants, taking a patient's reported symptoms and cross-referencing them with a vast database of medical knowledge to suggest potential diagnoses for a doctor to review.

In finance, high-frequency trading is dominated by AI agents that can monitor market trends and execute trades in fractions of a second, far faster than any human. These tools are also at the forefront of fraud detection. An AI agent can monitor your credit card transactions in real time, learning your typical spending patterns. If a transaction suddenly appears that deviates from your norm—for instance, a large purchase made in a different country—the agent can instantly flag it as potentially fraudulent and block the charge, protecting you from theft.

From streamlining operations to providing personalized assistance, AI agents are moving from theoretical concepts to indispensable tools that are reshaping our world.

Challenges and Considerations

While AI agents offer immense potential, organizations must address several challenges when contemplating their use:

- **Ethical Concerns:** Autonomous decision making requires guardrails to ensure responsible use.
- **Security:** AI agents often interact with sensitive data, making robust cybersecurity measures essential.
- **Integration:** Deploying AI agents requires seamless integration with existing tools and workflows.

From Models to Mature Systems: The Life Cycle of Traditional Machine Learning

While the potential of artificial intelligence is vast, the practical journey of implementing it within an organization follows a well-trodden, and often challenging, path. Examining the typical life cycle of a traditional machine learning project reveals common pitfalls and highlights the steps required to climb the ladder of AI maturity. This process is about more than algorithms and data: It aims to integrate intelligence into the very fabric of a business.

Stage 1. Anchoring to a Business Problem

Every successful machine learning project begins not with data, but rather with a question. The first and most critical step is *to identify a specific, measurable business problem* that needs solving. Without this clear anchor, a project risks becoming a purely academic exercise with no real-world impact. The goal is to move from a vague aspiration, such as "We want to use AI," to a concrete objective, such as "We need to reduce customer churn by 15% in the next fiscal year" or "We need to decrease equipment downtime on the factory floor by predicting mechanical failures a week in advance."

For example, a retail company might identify its business problem as inefficient inventory management, leading to both stockouts of popular items and overstocking of slow-moving products. This clear problem statement, "Optimize inventory to match demand," then becomes the guiding star for the entire project, defining what success will look like and which data will be needed.

Stage 2. Understanding the Value and Limits of the Data

With a clear problem defined, the focus shifts to the foundational ingredient of machine learning: data. This step takes a deep dive to *understand which data the organization possesses, where it resides, and what its potential value is*. Often, the discovery process reveals as much about the organization as it does about the data itself. A team might find a treasure trove of customer purchase histories, but realize the data is stored in disconnected silos with inconsistent formatting.

The value of the data is directly tied to the business problem. For a retail company trying to optimize its inventory, historical sales data is valuable, but it becomes exponentially more so when combined with data on marketing promotions, website traffic, and external factors such as local holidays and weather forecasts. Understanding these relationships and assessing the quality, completeness, accuracy, and biases of the data is paramount. A model trained on incomplete or biased data will not only be inaccurate, but also will actively make poor, and potentially costly, recommendations.

The Implementation Gap: Where Projects Falter

Many promising machine learning projects that excel in the first two stages of the maturity process ultimately fail to deliver lasting value. This failure often occurs in the final mile of implementation, where two critical aspects are frequently overlooked: the end-user experience (UI/UX) and the long-term operational life cycle.

All too often, *little or no thought is given to the UI/UX of the implementation*. For example, a data science team might spend months building a highly sophisticated model that predicts customer churn with 95% accuracy. However, if the output of this model is simply a raw spreadsheet of customer IDs and churn probabilities delivered once a week, it creates more work than it solves. How does a marketing manager use this list? Which customers should they contact first? What offers should they make? Without an intuitive interface and a dashboard that visualizes churn risk, integrates with the company's CRM software, and suggests targeted retention campaigns, the model's intelligence remains locked away, inaccessible to the very people who need it most.

Equally problematic is *lack of planning for continual monitoring and improvement*. A machine learning model is not a static piece of software. The world changes, and so does the data. A model trained to detect financial fraud will quickly become obsolete as criminals devise new tactics. This concept, known as "model drift," means that a model's accuracy will inevitably deteriorate over time unless it is constantly monitored and periodically retrained on new data. The traditional "build it and forget it" approach is a recipe for failure.

Charting Progress: The AI Maturity Scale

The ability of an organization to overcome these challenges and successfully integrate AI into its operations is a measure of its maturity. This journey can be understood as a progression through several distinct stages (Figure 5.4).

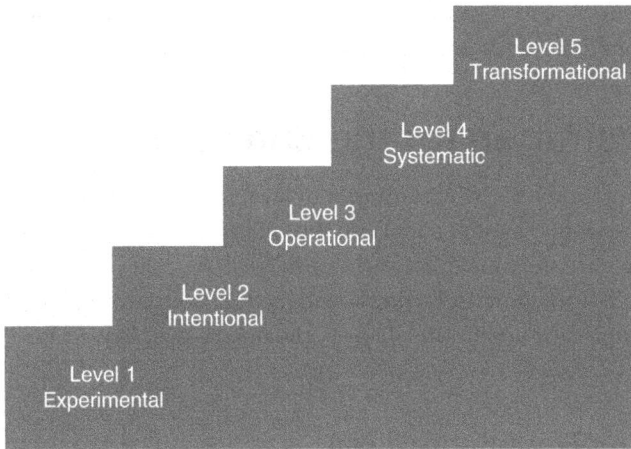

FIGURE 5.4 AI Maturity Steps

Here's a brief summary of these stages:

- **Level 1: Experimental.** At this initial stage, AI is explored in ad hoc "science projects." A single data scientist might build a model on their laptop to prove a concept. These projects are isolated from the business and rarely make it into production.

- **Level 2: Intentional.** The organization begins to strategically apply machine learning to specific, high-value problems. A few successful models might be deployed, but these efforts are often siloed within individual departments. The marketing team has its churn model, and the operations team has its forecasting model, but there is no shared infrastructure or strategy.

- **Level 3: Operational.** This is a major leap, marked by a focus on MLOps (machine learning operations). The organization builds pipelines to automate the deployment, monitoring, and retraining of models. The goal is to make AI reliable, repeatable, and robust.

- **Level 4: Systematic.** AI becomes a core, scalable business capability. The focus shifts to the end-user experience, ensuring that insights from models are delivered through intuitive applications. Common platforms and feature stores are built to allow different teams to share data and models, accelerating development and breaking down silos.

- **Level 5: Transformational.** At the highest level of maturity, the organization thinks "AI-first." It moves beyond using AI tools to make simple predictions to building autonomous agents that can make decisions and take action. The inventory management system doesn't just forecast demand; it analyzes supply chain risks, compares supplier pricing, and automatically places purchase orders to optimize

stock levels in real time. In this stage, AI is no longer just a tool; it is a fundamental driver of business operations and strategy.

AI Orchestration for the Enterprise

Scaling AI adoption at the organizational level is a completely different challenge from personal adoption. It requires not only technical expertise but also alignment between business strategy and employee enablement. Although most business leaders today recognize that AI is the future (and maybe even the present), the question is: *How do we implement AI effectively across our entire organization?*

Why AI Implementations Fail

Let's address the elephant in the room: *AI initiatives often fail to deliver their intended value.* While the reasons for this failure can vary, two common pitfalls stand out:

- **Chasing What's Hot:** Leaders can fall into the trap of adopting AI solutions simply because they're trendy, without fully understanding how these technologies align with their organization's strategy. For instance, an organization may invest in a cutting-edge AI model for predictive analytics without having the infrastructure or data quality to support it. **Impact:** These investments become expensive experiments that fail to deliver measurable results.

- **Overcomplicating the Solution:** On the technical side, teams can get caught up in using the most advanced tools and algorithms without considering the business objective. This often leads to overly complex systems that are difficult to maintain or scale. **Impact:** AI projects become disconnected from the organization's goals, leading to poor adoption and wasted resources.

Both leadership and technical teams share responsibility for these failures. The key to success lies in aligning goals, simplifying solutions, and maintaining a clear focus on outcomes.

The Quickest Win: Enabling Employees

The most effective way to integrate AI into your organization isn't starting with large-scale projects, but rather empowering your employees to become AI-enabled. This strategy offers two major advantages:

- **Quick Implementation:** Employees can begin using AI tools immediately, leading to rapid productivity gains.

- **Catching Up to Employees:** Many employees are already using AI, often without formal support or guidelines. Harnessing their enthusiasm while addressing gaps in security and knowledge sharing creates a strong foundation for enterprise-level AI adoption.

The Reality of AI Use Among Employees

Recent research highlights just how prevalent AI use already is among employees:

- 75% of knowledge workers use AI at work.
- 90% say it helps them focus on their most important work.
- 85% report feeling more creative and engaged with AI tools.

While these statistics are promising, they also reveal challenges:

- **Privacy and Security Risks:** Many employees bring their own AI tools to work, which can lead to sensitive data being shared with unapproved platforms. For example, a marketer might upload customer data into a generative AI tool without considering the compliance risks.
- **Knowledge Silos:** Employees may be reluctant to admit how they're using AI, due to either a fear of judgment or a desire to maintain a competitive edge within their team. In consequence, valuable insights are kept private, preventing the organization from scaling best practices.
- **Misuse of AI Tools:** Without clear guidelines, employees may unintentionally misuse AI tools, leading to ethical concerns or suboptimal results.

Leadership Must Act

For the first time, we're witnessing a major shift in technology adoption: Individual users are adopting AI tools faster than organizational leadership can develop policies or strategies for AI use. This grassroots adoption is exciting, but it also underscores the urgency for leaders to act.

A Microsoft report found that:

- 79% of leaders agree that adopting AI is critical to staying competitive.
- 59% of leaders worry about quantifying the productivity gains from AI.

This duality—recognizing AI's importance but feeling uncertain about its measurable impact—highlights the need for strategic planning.

To orchestrate AI adoption at scale, leaders must balance strategy with AI's technological capabilities, and support the organization's strategic vision by identifying the areas where AI can create the most value, from automating workflows to enhancing customer experiences. In addition, they must empower employees by providing tools, training, and a culture of experimentation to enable those employees to unlock AI's potential. By taking this dual approach, organizations can harness the grassroots enthusiasm for AI while building a structured, scalable framework for success.

Building a Strategic Plan for AI Enablement

To empower employees while also addressing organizational risks, leaders must take a proactive and structured approach to AI adoption.

The first step is to create a safe and secure AI environment. This involves implementing company-approved AI tools, which helps reduce reliance on unvetted or potentially risky platforms. It's equally important to provide training on privacy, compliance, and responsible AI usage to ensure employees are using these tools appropriately.

Next, organizations should foster a culture of knowledge sharing. This can be achieved by establishing forums or hosting workshops where employees are encouraged to present their AI use cases, highlight their successes, and reflect on lessons learned. Recognizing and rewarding innovative applications of AI further promotes transparency and collaboration across teams.

Another critical component is the development of clear guidelines. Organizations should establish policies that define acceptable AI use, outline data privacy requirements, and address ethical considerations. For instance, guidelines should clearly specify which types of data are permitted or restricted when using generative AI tools.

Finally, it's essential to measure and communicate the impact of AI initiatives. Leaders should define metrics that track improvements in productivity, creativity, and employee satisfaction resulting from AI use. Regularly sharing these insights with executive leadership can help demonstrate the value of AI, thereby building momentum and support for broader implementation across the organization.

Consider a global retail company in which employees across departments like marketing, operations, and customer support have already begun experimenting with generative AI tools. They've been using these tools to write marketing copy, analyze sales trends, and respond more efficiently to customer inquiries. Recognizing this organic adoption, leadership decides to formalize the approach by launching an AI enablement program.

The program introduces company-approved tools, such as Jasper for content creation and UiPath for automation, ensuring employees have access to secure, reliable platforms. To promote ongoing learning and collaboration, the company also hosts monthly "AI Power Hours," providing a space where team members can share practical tips and real-world use cases. In addition, an internal knowledge base is developed, offering a centralized hub of AI tools, best practices, and usage guidelines, helping to scale AI adoption safely and strategically across the organization.

Within six months, the company sees measurable improvements in efficiency and employee engagement while mitigating the risks related to privacy and misuse.

Level Setting

Leaders and organizations achieving real results with AI enablement have one thing in common: They start by **level setting**, ensuring everyone understands what AI is, as well as what it can and cannot do, and addressing its limitations and risks openly.

The Importance of Starting the Conversation

AI's presence in the mainstream conversation is undeniable. Just yesterday, I was in the grocery store and spotted an entire magazine dedicated to AI. Seeing it alongside *Time* and *People* magazines filled me with excitement, it was a moment of realization: "We made it! AI is no longer a niche topic; it's part of everyday life."

That said, it's important to remember that while AI is now mainstream, the level of understanding among your employees will vary widely. *Some will be cautious*, worrying about risks like job displacement, ethical concerns, or the misuse of AI. *Others will be enthusiastic adopters*, who are already integrating AI into their workflows and excited about the possibilities.

This disparity in understanding and attitudes can lead to misalignment, confusion, and even resistance. By opening the dialogue with a **level-setting conversation**, you create a shared foundation for understanding AI across your organization.

How to Level-Set Effectively

When introducing AI to your team, it's important to start with a clear and simple definition. Explain that AI is a tool designed to analyze data, make predictions, and assist with various tasks. However, it is not capable of independent thinking or human-like creativity. Help make this distinction concrete by offering examples, such as AI tools' ability to generate text or identify patterns, and clarifying what AI cannot do, such as making moral judgments or strategic decisions on its own.

It is equally important to acknowledge the risks and limitations of AI. Address common concerns directly, including issues around privacy, data security, and algorithmic bias. Reassure your team by outlining your organization's ethical standards and the safeguards in place to ensure responsible AI use. Transparency in this area will help build trust.

Once the risks are addressed, highlight the many opportunities AI presents. Show how it can improve productivity, spark new ideas, and free up time for employees to focus on more meaningful, high-value work. Use familiar, practical examples such as AI tools that automate email organization or assist in generating marketing content to help these benefits feel tangible.

Finally, create space for open dialogue. Encourage employees to voice their questions or concerns without fear of judgment. Invite them to share how they are already experimenting with AI in their roles. This not only fosters a sense of inclusion but also promotes peer learning and collaboration as your organization grows more confident in its AI journey.

Example: A Successful Level-Setting Conversation

A mid-sized retail company recently held an AI town hall to introduce its employees to the organization's AI strategy. The session included the following components:

- A clear explanation of AI's capabilities and limitations
- A panel discussion in which employees who were early adopters of AI tools shared how they used AI to save time and solve problems

- An anonymous Q&A session where employees could ask questions without fear of judgment

The result? Employees left the session with greater clarity, excitement, and alignment on the organization's AI goals.

Quantify and Assess

Once the organization has a shared understanding of AI's capabilities, the next critical step is to quantify and assess the baseline. Unfortunately, many organizations skip this step, often to their detriment. Without understanding where you are starting from, it's impossible to measure progress or determine where AI will have the greatest impact.

A data-driven approach ensures that:

- AI initiatives are aligned with real business needs, not just trends or assumptions.
- Training and tools are tailored to specific roles and tasks, maximizing relevance and adoption.

At the Human Machine Collaboration Institute, we have pioneered a systematic method for seamlessly integrating AI into an organization's existing structure. Our approach begins with a detailed analysis of the job descriptions for every role within the organization. We meticulously break down these descriptions into their constituent individual tasks. Each task is then carefully evaluated to determine the potential for AI intervention, which we classify into three levels: AI assistance, partial automation, or full automation. By aggregating this task-level data, we construct a comprehensive map that reveals the landscape of AI potential across the entire organization. This strategic overview typically highlights that 35% to 45% of tasks within any given role can be supported by AI and uncovers patterns across departments, pinpointing specific roles and workflows ripe for AI integration.

Such a granular assessment yields multiple strategic advantages. First, it allows for the development of tailored training programs. Instead of generic AI education, employees receive instruction that is directly relevant to their specific roles and daily tasks. For instance, marketing teams can be trained on leveraging generative AI for content creation, while finance teams can focus on AI applications for forecasting and process automation. Second, this detailed understanding enables leadership to make targeted tool selections, ensuring that any new software, such as a CRM system with AI capabilities or a sophisticated data analytics platform, directly aligns with the organization's identified needs. Lastly, when the organization has a clear picture of where and how AI will be applied, establishing precise and effective guidelines for its use becomes a more straightforward and efficient process.

Example: Quantifying AI Opportunities

A healthcare organization conducted a task analysis across its departments to explore where AI could add the most value. The findings were illuminating. In administrative roles, about 60% of tasks, such as scheduling and billing, were identified as candidates for automation through RPA and AI agents. In clinical roles, approximately 30% of tasks, including patient monitoring and report generation, were found to benefit from AI augmentation rather than full automation.

With this data in hand, the organization moved quickly. It implemented RPA tools to handle repetitive administrative tasks, which allowed staff to redirect their time toward more meaningful work such as direct patient care. On the clinical side, it equipped healthcare providers with AI-powered diagnostic tools to assist in decision making and improve patient outcomes.

Steps to Quantify and Assess AI Opportunities

As just described, the process of quantifying AI opportunities begins with a clear task inventory. This means documenting the specific tasks performed by employees across different roles to understand the day-to-day functions of the organization.

Next, evaluate each task for AI compatibility. This assessment considers factors such as how repetitive the task is, how complex it may be, and whether it requires human judgment. Tasks that are routine and rules-based are often ideal candidates for automation. By comparison, tasks that involve nuance or creativity may be better suited for AI-assisted augmentation.

Once the evaluation is complete, the organization should prioritize the opportunities. The most impactful opportunities usually lie in high-frequency tasks that drain time or resources. For instance, automating report generation or handling common customer inquiries often delivers quick wins.

Finally, it's essential to define metrics for success. Establishing clear key performance indicators—for example, time saved, cost reductions, or improvements in employee satisfaction—provides a way to measure AI's impact and refine the approach over time.

By combining level-setting conversations with this kind of quantified task analysis, organizations can create a solid foundation for AI adoption. This method keeps employees informed and involved, while enabling leaders to make smart, data-driven decisions that lead to real, measurable results.

AI Guidelines and Policies

One of the most common missteps organizations make when adopting AI is creating a rigid policy before they even know which tools they will use or how those tools will be applied. This is analogous to installing stop signs before you've built the road. Sure, you want to prevent accidents, but without knowing where the road leads or how it will be used, your stop signs may end up being useless or, even worse, counterproductive.

The same applies to AI policy. If policies are established before you've fully assessed your organization's needs and chosen your tools, they can create unnecessary restrictions, stifle innovation, and fail to address real concerns.

Before drafting any policies, organizations must complete the critical step of quantifying and assessing. As discussed earlier, this process helps identify where AI will be used (which roles, tasks, and workflows can benefit most from AI) and which tools are needed (e.g., generative AI for content creation, RPA for task automation, AI agents for customer service). Only after this groundwork is laid can policies and guidelines be tailored to your organization's specific use cases.

Guidelines Versus Policies

Although policies are essential for maintaining compliance and safeguarding your organization, they can be difficult to keep updated in a rapidly evolving landscape like AI. This is why I recommend a dual approach, consisting of (1) flexible guidelines and (2) privacy and security policies.

- **Flexible Guidelines**
    - **Purpose:** Provide employees with a clear framework for using AI tools responsibly while allowing room for adaptation.

- **Key Components:**
  - Examples of appropriate AI use (e.g., content creation, data analysis)
  - Areas where AI use is restricted (e.g., handling sensitive data)
  - Best practices for maximizing AI's potential while minimizing risks
- **Why They Work:** Guidelines can evolve alongside the technology, ensuring employees have up-to-date recommendations without waiting for formal policy updates.

- **Privacy and Security Policies**
  - **Purpose:** Protect sensitive data and ensure compliance with regulations like the European Union's General Data Protection Regulation (GDPR), the Health Portability and Accountability Act (HIPAA), or the California Consumer Privacy Act (CCPA).
  - **Key Components:**
    - Clear restrictions on how sensitive data can be handled by AI tools
    - Requirements for vetting third-party AI platforms to ensure they meet security standards
    - Training programs to educate employees on cybersecurity risks specific to AI

Guidelines: Why Flexibility Is Key

The rapid pace of AI advancements means that what works today may not work tomorrow. By emphasizing flexible guidelines over rigid policies, organizations can stay agile, empowering employees to innovate while maintaining control and security. This approach ensures that AI tools are used effectively, responsibly, and in ways that align with your organization's goals and values.

Policies: Why Privacy and Security Are Non-Negotiable

As the adoption of AI becomes more widespread, concerns surrounding privacy and security are naturally intensifying. Many organizations have already established policies and annual employee training programs for these critical areas. However, if your organization has not yet formalized these protocols, the growing integration of AI makes it imperative to do so now.

A proactive approach involves several key steps. First, it is essential to audit your current privacy and security policies to determine whether they adequately address AI-specific risks, such as the potential for employees to input sensitive company data into external generative AI models. Following this assessment, employees should receive practical, scenario-based training that prepares them for AI-related threats, including sophisticated phishing scams that leverage AI-generated content, and the risk of accidental data leaks through AI tools. To ensure their privacy and security policies are effective, organizations can use AI-powered solutions to monitor compliance in real time, automatically flagging potential breaches or the misuse of approved tools.

These policies are not merely theoretical: They have tangible applications across various sectors. For instance, a retail company might permit its marketing team to use generative AI for creating ad copy but mandate that a human editor review and approve all outputs before they are published. In a more sensitive context, a financial institution could strictly prohibit its employees from entering any customer financial data into third-party AI platforms, opting instead to develop and use a secure, approved in-house AI system. Similarly, a telecommunications company could deploy AI agents to handle routine customer inquiries while using sophisticated monitoring tools to ensure the agents adhere to pre-approved scripts and correctly escalate sensitive issues to human representatives.

Best Practices for Developing AI Guidelines and Policies

To establish effective AI guidelines and policies, the first step is to start with a comprehensive use-case inventory. This requires documenting all current applications of AI within the organization, including informal or shadow IT uses. While creating this inventory, it is beneficial to actively engage with employees, encouraging them to share their experiences. That can help to identify existing pain points, potential risks, and organic innovations that are already taking place.

A foundational element of any AI policy is the prioritization of privacy and security. This requires close collaboration with data governance and cybersecurity teams to update existing privacy policies, ensuring they explicitly address the nuances of AI. For example, one critical guideline would be to prohibit the uploading of sensitive data, such as customer records or proprietary information, to public generative AI tools that may store or share user inputs. This guideline aims to prevent potential data breaches.

While setting boundaries is important, guidelines should also foster a culture of responsible experimentation. Policies should encourage employees to explore the capabilities of AI to discover new efficiencies and applications, while simultaneously emphasizing ethical consider-ations and responsible usage. For example, the organization could offer practical tips, such as mandating the double-checking of AI-generated outputs for accuracy and cautioning against over-reliance on AI for critical decision making without human oversight.

One practical approach is to create tiered policies, as different roles and departments will interact with AI in distinct ways, necessitating varying levels of oversight. For instance, guidelines for marketing teams might focus on the ethical creation of content and the transparent use of social media automation. In contrast, finance teams would require much stricter policies centered on data security, accuracy, and adherence to regulatory compliance when using AI for financial modeling or analysis.

Figure 5.5 summarizes the recommended approach to take when creating AI policies and guidelines.

AI Guidelines and Policies

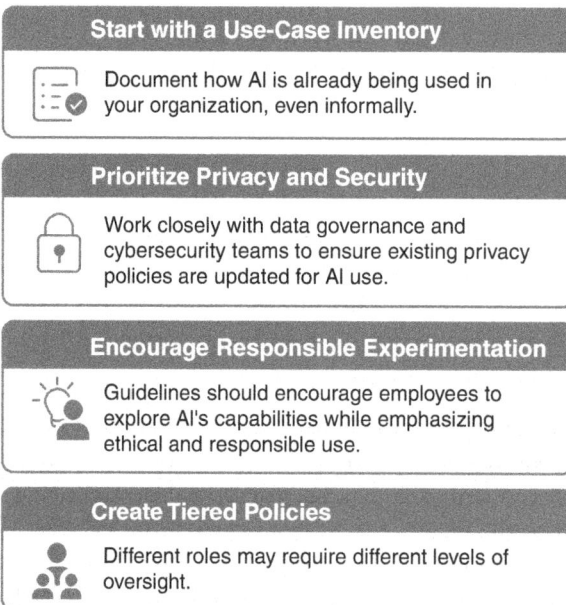

Start with a Use-Case Inventory

Document how AI is already being used in your organization, even informally.

Prioritize Privacy and Security

Work closely with data governance and cybersecurity teams to ensure existing privacy policies are updated for AI use.

Encourage Responsible Experimentation

Guidelines should encourage employees to explore AI's capabilities while emphasizing ethical and responsible use.

Create Tiered Policies

Different roles may require different levels of oversight.

FIGURE 5.5 AI Guidelines and Policies

AI is a rapidly evolving field, so guidelines and policies must be treated as living documents. Organizations should schedule regular reviews, perhaps every six months, to ensure that their policies remain relevant and effective. These periodic updates allow the organization to account for new tools, technological advancements, and valuable employee feedback, ensuring governance keeps pace with innovation.

Training

The abundance of online classes and resources for learning AI is both a blessing and a curse. From massive open online courses (MOOCs) like those offered by Coursera and LinkedIn Learning to niche platforms and YouTube tutorials, there's no shortage of material. But the real challenge isn't finding a class: It's finding the *right training for the right person at the right time.*

Platforms like Coursera and LinkedIn are excellent options for democratizing education, and I've had the privilege of teaching on both. Unfortunately, many of these courses fall short when it comes to enabling learners to apply their knowledge quickly and effectively.

Tailored Training: Start with Assessment

The most effective training programs begin with a clear understanding of the learner's needs. This means conducting an initial assessment to identify:

- **The Learner's Role and Responsibilities:** What tasks do they perform daily, and how might AI assist?
- **Their Current Proficiency:** Are they new to AI, or have they already experimented with tools?
- **Specific Goals:** What outcomes do they want to achieve with AI, and how will this align with organizational goals?

This assessment informs a tailored training approach that provides:

- **Role-Specific Learning:** A marketing professional might focus on using generative AI for content creation, while a financial analyst would prioritize automation and data analysis tools.
- **Actionable Insights:** Instead of long theoretical lectures, learners get concise, practical knowledge they can apply immediately.

Hands-On Experience Is Key

The best way to learn AI is by *using it in real-world scenarios*. Training programs should balance formal education with hands-on experimentation, encouraging employees to explore tools such as the following:

- Generative AI platforms for drafting emails or creating social media posts
- RPA tools to automate repetitive tasks like scheduling or data transfers
- AI analytics platforms to extract insights from large datasets

Short, actionable modules, combined with real-world practice, ensure employees spend more time applying what they've learned and less time passively consuming information.

Fostering a Learning Community

Another critical component of effective training is building a *community of learners within your organization*. A thriving AI community fosters collaboration, inspiration, and shared learning. Here's how to create one:

- **Internal User Groups:** Establish forums or regular meetings where employees can discuss how they're using AI, share success stories, and troubleshoot challenges.
- **AI Champions:** Identify early adopters or employees with strong AI skills to serve as mentors, offering guidance and encouragement to others.
- **Knowledge-Sharing Platforms:** Use tools like Slack, Microsoft Teams, or internal wikis to create a centralized hub for AI tips, use cases, and training materials.

This community-driven approach creates a feedback loop: As employees experiment with AI tools, they share their findings, which inspires others to try new things.

Continual Empowerment

AI tools and models are evolving at an unprecedented pace. Language models are being updated every four to eight months, and advancements in multimodal models are arriving just as quickly. This rapid progression makes *continual empowerment* essential.

Ongoing Learning and Development

To keep pace with these changes, organizations must provide employees with opportunities for ongoing education. This includes the following:

- **Regular Training Updates**
  - Offer bite-sized modules or microlearning sessions that cover the latest features, tools, or techniques.
  - Example: A 15-minute session on new capabilities in a generative AI platform like GPT or Midjourney.
- **Refresher Courses**
  - Periodically revisit foundational topics to ensure employees remain confident in their skills.
  - Example: A quarterly workshop on improving prompt engineering for better AI outputs.
- **Community-Led Updates**
  - Encourage employees to share updates on tools they've explored or techniques they've mastered.

Dynamic Guidelines and Policies

Continual empowerment isn't just about training; it's about adapting organizational guidelines and policies to reflect new realities. As models and tools evolve, the policies around their use must evolve, too. This includes:

- Updating security protocols to account for new data-sharing risks.
- Revising guidelines to incorporate newly released features or applications.
- Conducting periodic reviews to assess how employees are implementing AI and identifying areas for improvement.

Measuring Progress

Regularly assessing progress ensures that employees stay engaged and that training programs deliver value. Consider these approaches:

- **Skill Assessments:** Use surveys or quizzes to evaluate employees' confidence and competence in using AI tools.
- **Impact Metrics:** Measure the tangible benefits of training, such as time saved, productivity gains, and improved employee satisfaction.
- **Feedback Loops:** Gather input from employees about what's working and where they need more support.

Example: A Continual Empowerment Program in Action

Here's an example of a continual empowerment program in action at a government organization. This organization implemented a robust AI training and empowerment initiative that began by providing employees with training tailored to their specific roles, creating distinct modules for departments like marketing, operations, and product development. To maintain momentum and foster a culture of discovery, the organization hosted monthly "AI Power Hours," which created a dedicated space for employees to explore new tools and share practical use cases with their colleagues. This hands-on approach was supported by dynamic guidelines that ensured employees stayed informed about the latest security protocols and best practices. Finally, quarterly reviews provided leadership with crucial data on the program's impact, allowing them to make informed decisions and refine future training initiatives. The result of this comprehensive strategy was a workforce that felt confident using AI, leading to soaring adoption rates and measurable productivity gains for the organization.

The success of this program highlights several key points for any organization looking to build a training and empowerment strategy. It is essential to tailor the training by first assessing individual and departmental needs to provide role-specific education. A top priority should be hands-on learning, where employees are encouraged to experiment directly with AI tools and apply their new skills in real-world contexts.

Building a sense of community is also crucial: Fostering collaboration and knowledge-sharing among employees helps accelerate learning and innovation. Because the AI field is changing so rapidly, it is vital to embrace continuous learning by providing regular updates and adapting guidelines to keep pace with new advancements. To ensure the continual empowerment program is effective, organizations must measure its impact, using clear metrics to evaluate success and identify areas for improvement.

By taking a dynamic, community-driven approach to training and empowerment, organizations can ensure employees remain confident, skilled, and prepared to leverage AI effectively.

Measuring Impact

Measuring the impact of AI adoption and training is a critical, yet often overlooked, aspect of successful implementation. While establishing a baseline is essential, the real value lies in understanding how AI tools transform workflows, enhance creativity, and enable employees to focus on what matters most. These insights can guide organizations in reallocating resources, optimizing processes, and identifying opportunities for new initiatives.

Why Measuring Impact Matters

Without measurable outcomes, it's difficult to determine whether AI tools and training programs are really delivering their intended value. By quantifying the impact, organizations can achieve the following goals:

- **Validate Return on Investment (ROI):** Demonstrate the financial benefits of AI tools and programs.
- **Identify Areas for Improvement:** Pinpoint workflows or training modules that need refinement.
- **Foster Confidence:** Share tangible results with employees and leadership to build momentum for continued AI adoption.

Key Metrics to Measure AI Enablement at Scale

The following metrics provide a comprehensive view of AI's impact on organizational performance.

Employee-Centric Metrics

Employee-centric metrics include the following:

1. **Ability to Focus on Important Work**
   - **What to Measure:** The percentage of time employees spend on high-value, strategic tasks versus routine or repetitive ones.
   - **Why It Matters:** AI should enable employees to prioritize meaningful work, reducing distractions and task-switching.
   - **Example:** A marketing team reports a 30% increase in time spent brainstorming and executing campaigns, thanks to AI automating its email scheduling and report generation.

2. **Speed to Get Unstuck Within a Project**
   - **What to Measure:** The average time employees take to overcome bottlenecks or obstacles using AI tools.
   - **Why It Matters:** AI tools should act as problem-solving accelerators, allowing employees to maintain momentum.

- **Example:** A software developer uses an AI coding assistant to debug issues in half the time it previously took.

3. **Employee Overall Fulfillment in Work**

   - **What to Measure:** Employee satisfaction, engagement, and sense of accomplishment.

   - **Why It Matters:** Fulfillment indicates whether AI tools are reducing burnout and enabling employees to find more joy in their work.

   - **How to Measure:** Use employee surveys or engagement scores.

4. **Time Savings on Tasks**

   - **What to Measure:** The reduction in time required to complete specific tasks after AI implementation.

   - **Why It Matters:** Time savings directly translate into increased productivity and capacity for innovation.

   - **Example:** A finance team cuts the time needed to create quarterly forecasts by 40% using AI-powered tools.

5. **Problem-Solving Efficiency**

   - **What to Measure:** The average time it takes employees to find solutions to challenges using AI tools.

   - **Why It Matters:** Problem solving is a core benefit of AI, empowering employees to think creatively and act decisively.

Organizational Metrics

Organizational metrics include the following:

6. **Tangible Outcomes from AI Enablement**

   - **What to Measure:** Specific, measurable results achieved through AI, such as increased sales, reduced errors, or improved customer satisfaction.

   - **Example:** A customer service team resolves 25% more tickets per week using AI chatbots.

7. **Task Automation Rate**

   - **What to Measure:** The percentage of tasks automated using AI tools.

   - **Why It Matters:** This metric highlights where AI has reduced manual effort, freeing up resources for other priorities.

   - **Example:** An HR department automates 50% of its candidate screening process with AI tools.

8. **Return on Investment**

   - **What to Measure:** The financial return generated by AI tools and training programs relative to their cost.

   - **Why It Matters:** ROI demonstrates the tangible value of AI adoption to both leadership and stakeholders.

Strategic Metrics

Strategic metrics include the following:

9. **Combined Intelligence Score**

   - **What to Measure:** The overall enhancement in organizational intelligence, reflecting how effectively humans and AI are collaborating.

   - **Why It Matters:** This metric tracks whether AI is augmenting human capabilities in a meaningful way.

10. **Cost of Intelligence**

    - **What to Measure:** The financial cost of implementing and maintaining AI tools relative to the value they deliver.

    - **Why It Matters:** This ensures that AI initiatives are cost-effective and scalable.

11. **Reallocation of Resources**

    - **What to Measure:** Changes in resource allocation due to efficiencies gained from AI.

    - **Why It Matters:** Highlighting resource shifts, such as reallocation of team members from data entry to strategic planning, underscores AI's transformative potential.

Steps to Measure Impact

Follow these steps to measure the impact that AI is having on your organization:

1. **Set a Baseline**

   - Before implementing AI tools or training programs, establish benchmarks for the metrics you plan to track. For example, measure current task completion times, employee satisfaction scores, and manual effort rates.

2. **Monitor Progress Regularly**

   - Track metrics at regular intervals (e.g., monthly or quarterly) to assess the ongoing impact of AI.

3. Use Tools to Measure Metrics

- Leverage analytics tools and dashboards to gather and visualize data. For example:
  - Use employee feedback platforms like Culture Amp to measure engagement.
  - Deploy workflow tools like Asana or Jira to track task completion times.

4. Gather Qualitative Feedback

- Metrics alone don't tell the whole story. Conduct interviews or focus groups with employees to understand their experiences with AI tools.

5. Iterate and Refine

- Use your findings to adjust training programs, reallocate resources, or refine AI tool implementations.

Example: Measuring AI Impact in a Retail Organization

A retail company introduced AI in an effort to optimize its inventory management and customer support. It tracked the following metrics:

- **Task Automation Rate:** 40% of manual inventory updates were automated, reducing errors by 25%.
- **Tangible Outcomes:** Customer wait times decreased by 30% thanks to AI chatbots.
- **Employee Fulfillment:** Surveys showed a 20% increase in job satisfaction, as employees spent less time on repetitive tasks.

These insights helped the company allocate more resources to strategic initiatives, such as expanding into new markets, while improving its overall efficiency.

Key Takeaways for Measuring Impact

Key considerations when measuring the impact of AI within your organization include the following:

- Define metrics that align with your organization's goals.
- Establish a baseline before implementation to track meaningful progress.
- Combine quantitative metrics (e.g., ROI, time savings) with qualitative insights (e.g., employee feedback).

- Iterate based on your findings to maximize the value of the AI tools and training.

By making measurement an integral part of your AI strategy, you ensure that your organization isn't just adopting AI, it's truly benefiting from it.

Conclusion: From Personal Practice to Organizational Strategy

This chapter explored the multifaceted journey of becoming an AI Orchestrator—a path marked by curiosity, strategic implementation, and continuous learning. This journey begins not with a massive corporate initiative, but rather with personal orchestration. It starts with understanding your own patterns and workflows, and identifying where AI can automate tasks and amplify creativity. This individual mastery forms the essential foundation upon which broader organizational change is built.

As this practice scales, it becomes crucial to foster open conversations across the organization. Leaders must proactively address the fears and misconceptions surrounding AI, creating a shared, foundational understanding that builds trust and encourages collaboration. This transparency must be paired with a data-driven approach, where needs are quantified and assessed to ensure AI tools and training are targeted where they can deliver the most value.

Given the rapid evolution of AI models, a one-time workshop is not enough to ensure the organization maximizes AI's benefits. Organizations must commit to enabling continuous learning by providing ongoing education, fostering communities of practice, and adapting policies as technology advances. Ultimately, sustained success hinges on the ability to measure, reflect, and iterate. By tracking key metrics—which can range from productivity gains to ROI—leaders can prove the value of their investment and intelligently refine their strategies over time.

In Chapter 6, we will scale these principles across the entire enterprise and consider how to build AI-driven ecosystems in which human ingenuity and machine intelligence work in seamless partnership. The potential of AI is not merely about efficiency; it's about reimagining how we work, create, and solve problems. By embracing the principles of orchestration, we can transform our workflows and redefine innovation itself. The future of work is here, and AI is the catalyst for the journey.

6

Ethical Machines

Whenever we encounter new technologies like AI, their potential often feels like holding a double-edged sword. On the one hand, these technologies can lead to groundbreaking advancements, solving some of humanity's most pressing challenges. On the other hand, they carry risks—some obvious and others unforeseen. History has shown that innovation often comes with unintended consequences, and AI is no different. This chapter unpacks the ethical dilemmas surrounding intelligent machines and explores how we can navigate these challenges responsibly. Most importantly, it aims to equip you with the knowledge to engage with AI in a way that aligns with your values and contributes positively to the world.

What Is Ethics?

Before we dive into the ethical concerns related to AI, it's important to pause and think about the concept of ethics itself. The *Longman Dictionary* defines **ethics** as "a general idea or belief that influences people's behavior and attitudes." That framing shifts our perspective: Ethics aren't just rigid rules or abstract theories, but guiding beliefs that shape how individuals and societies act. This raises deeper questions: What beliefs most influence our behavior? Are they uniquely human, or could a computer system be designed to reflect or even emulate them? And, perhaps most critically, do machines need guiding ideas or beliefs to operate in a way we consider responsible?

To explore these questions, it's important to first reflect on our own morals and values. As individuals, our morals are shaped by culture, upbringing, and personal experience. They represent the principles that guide how we judge right from wrong. Values, in contrast, reflect what we prioritize in life, whether it's family, freedom, creativity, or community.

AI, as a technology, has no inherent sense of right or wrong. However, the systems we build reflect the morals and values of the people and organizations creating them. That's why understanding your own ethical compass is an essential first step in engaging responsibly with AI.

Exercise: Defining Your Morals and Values

Take a moment to pause and reflect. This exercise will help you clarify your own guiding principles and priorities. It takes only a few minutes, but the insights could shape how you approach AI and technology more broadly.

Step 1: Identify Your Morals

Write down the principles you believe are essential for living an ethical life. These might include:

- **Honesty:** Being truthful and transparent in your actions.
- **Respect:** Treating others with dignity and fairness.
- **Integrity:** Staying true to your values even when it's difficult.
- **Compassion:** Empathizing with others and showing kindness.
- **Justice:** Striving for fairness and equality in all situations.

Step 2: Clarify Your Values

Now, write down the things you prioritize in your life. These might include:

- **Family:** Nurturing close relationships with loved ones.
- **Freedom:** Valuing autonomy and self-determination.
- **Health:** Prioritizing physical and mental well-being.
- **Creativity:** Pursuing innovation and self-expression.
- **Community:** Supporting others and contributing to society.

Step 3: Reflect

Look at your lists. Do any of the morals and values overlap or complement each other? For example, if honesty is a moral and trust is a value, they likely reinforce each other. How might these morals and values influence the way you approach decisions, technology, or even AI?

The Gray Area: Morals, Values, and Machines

Now that you've considered your own morals and values, let's return to the question asked earlier: Can intelligent machines have morals and values? At first glance, that seems impossible. After all, machines lack consciousness, emotion, and cultural context. Yet, when we design AI systems, we program them to emulate certain values, even if indirectly. For example:

- A healthcare AI prioritizing patient safety reflects a moral principle of "do no harm."
- A recommendation algorithm suggesting diverse content mirrors values like inclusivity and fairness.

This raises a fascinating dilemma. Although machines cannot possess values, their behavior can reflect them. The challenge lies in ensuring those reflections align with human ethics, especially given the diversity of values across cultures, professions, and individuals. For example:

- What happens when a company's profit-driven values conflict with societal concerns like fairness or privacy?
- How do we ensure that an AI system is flexible enough to respect individual preferences while adhering to universal principles?

These are complex questions without easy answers. But as users and creators of AI, we play a critical role in guiding how these technologies are designed, deployed, and held accountable.

Framing the Ethical Landscape

Ethical questions often arise when a mismatch occurs between what we expect of technology and what it delivers. For example:

• **Trust:** If an AI system fails to act transparently, can we trust its decisions?

• **Bias:** If a machine learning model inherits biased data, can it act fairly?

• **Control:** How do we maintain oversight when AI systems grow more autonomous?

Each of these concerns ties back to core ethical principles. By understanding our own ethics, we can better evaluate how AI aligns—or misaligns—with the values we hold dear.

Levels of Risk

To effectively assess the risks associated with AI, it's important to differentiate between **narrow AI** (often called "weak AI") and **artificial general intelligence** (AGI). Narrow AI excels in specific, clearly defined tasks—think of chatbots, facial recognition, or fraud detection systems. AGI, by contrast, represents the hypothetical leap to machines that can outperform humans across a wide array of cognitive tasks, from problem solving to creative reasoning.

AGI is a concept that has yet to be fully realized. Nevertheless, it dominates much of the ethical discourse around AI because of the profound implications it carries.

Performance Levels: Narrow AI Versus AGI

Google's DeepMind provides a helpful framework for understanding AI performance levels:

• **Level 1 (Emerging):** Comparable to an unskilled human.

• **Level 2 (Competent):** Matches the 50th percentile of skilled adults.

• **Level 3 (Expert):** Surpasses 90% of skilled adults.

• **Level 4 (Virtuoso):** Outperforms 99% of skilled adults.

• **Level 5 (Superhuman):** Exceeds the capabilities of all humans.

When it comes to narrow AI, we have already reached and surpassed superhuman performance in many domains. For example, AI systems can outpace human experts in tasks like protein folding (AlphaFold), playing chess and Go (AlphaZero), and parsing massive datasets to identify patterns. These achievements, while remarkable, remain task-specific. The leap to AGI, where machines could seamlessly apply intelligence across multiple domains, has proved far more elusive. By most accounts, we have reached Level 1 on the AGI scale, barely scratching the surface.

Understanding the distinction between narrow AI and AGI is crucial for meaningful discussions about ethics and risk. Narrow AI presents immediate, tangible challenges, while AGI stirs more abstract fears rooted in the unknown.

The Fear of Losing Control

Among the most profound concerns surrounding AGI is the fear of losing human control. This anxiety is deeply ingrained in our evolutionary history. For millennia, humans have relied on intelligence as their primary survival mechanism. We may not be the fastest or strongest species, but our ability to create tools, collaborate, and adapt has allowed us to thrive. The idea of creating a machine that could surpass us intellectually challenges this long-held belief in our unique dominance.

This fear has often been magnified by popular culture. Films like *The Matrix*, *2001: A Space Odyssey*, *I, Robot*, and *The Terminator* dramatize scenarios in which humanity is subjugated, or outright eradicated, by the very technologies we created. These narratives tap into our primal fear of being replaced, whether by a superior species or, in the case of AI, a superior intelligence.

Even so, humans have a paradoxical view of AI. While we dread the idea of losing control to intelligent machines, we eagerly delegate our mundane tasks to them. From letting AI sort our emails to relying on navigation apps, we're quick to offload our cognitive burdens to technology. We want to shed the tedium of everyday work but are reluctant to relinquish control entirely. This duality highlights the crux of our relationship with AI: a tension between efficiency and autonomy.

The Singularity: A Hypothesized Point of No Return

One of the most provocative ideas surrounding AGI is the concept of the **technological singularity**, popularized by futurist Ray Kurzweil in his book *The Singularity Is Near*. Kurzweil predicts that by 2045, technological progress will reach a tipping point where advances occur so rapidly that predicting outcomes becomes impossible. This would represent a phase where machines not only surpass human intelligence but also continuously improve themselves at an accelerating pace.

Kurzweil's theory isn't just about speed; it's about *exponential growth*. Consider how the time between industrial revolutions has progressively shortened: The First Industrial Revolution, centered on steam power, took nearly 120 years to evolve into the Second Industrial Revolution, based on electrical power. The transition to the digital era of computers occurred within decades. Today, AI advancements seem to emerge every six months.

This acceleration has fueled both optimism and unease. On the one hand, it promises breakthroughs in healthcare, climate solutions, and productivity. On the other hand, it stirs fears about humanity's ability to control or even comprehend what lies on the other side of such rapid progress.

Narrow AI Risks: Where the Immediate Concerns Lie

While AGI both captures the human imagination and stokes existential dread, the most pressing risks today are linked to narrow AI. These systems, despite their limitations, are already deeply embedded in our lives, from judicial algorithms to hiring tools. Ethical challenges in narrow AI often stem from the following concerns:

- **Bias and Fairness:** AI systems trained on flawed or incomplete data can perpetuate systemic inequalities.
- **Hallucinations and Misinformation:** Generative AI can confidently produce plausible but incorrect or harmful content.
- **Transparency and Accountability:** Many AI systems operate as "black boxes," making their decision-making processes difficult to understand or challenge.

For example, if it was trained on biased historical data, an AI model used in hiring might favor candidates from a specific demographic. If prompted incorrectly, a generative AI model might confidently generate inaccurate medical advice. These risks underscore the need for ethical oversight and informed usage.

Becoming a Knowledgeable Conductor of AI

As AI Orchestrators, we must learn to treat these systems as instruments in a symphony. Just as a conductor understands the range and limitations of each musician, so we must understand the scope and constraints of our AI tools. Here are some principles to guide this approach:

- **Understand the Boundaries:** Know what your AI tools can and cannot do. Recognize that the narrow AI system might be powerful in its domain but lacks the flexibility of human reasoning.
- **Double-Check Outputs:** Even the most advanced systems require human oversight to catch errors, bias, or hallucinations.
- **Educate and Empower:** Equip yourself and others with the knowledge to use AI responsibly, ensuring its strengths are harnessed while its risks are mitigated.

The responsibility of managing AI doesn't lie solely with developers. As users and decision makers, we also play a critical role in shaping how these systems are implemented and integrated. By staying informed and vigilant, we can ensure AI enhances—not diminishes—our human potential.

Narrow AI's Limitations and Challenges

Understanding these risks is crucial for anyone who uses or interacts with AI. Three key challenges stand out in this realm: hallucinations and false information, bias and fairness, and transparency and explainability. The following sections explore these challenges in depth.

Hallucinations and False Information

In the context of generative AI, a "hallucination" refers to instances in which the model generates content that sounds plausible but is factually incorrect, misleading, or nonsensical. These hallucinations pose significant risks, particularly when AI is used for critical applications such as decision making, summarizing research, or providing medical advice. Let's break down the factors that contribute to these errors.

Training Data Quality

Generative AI models are trained on massive datasets sourced from the Internet, including books, articles, and online conversations. Although this breadth enables versatility, the quality of this data varies widely.

In consequence, outdated, incorrect, or biased information can become part of the model's "knowledge base."

For example, when Google launched its AI-powered search, it made headlines for claiming that "eating rocks is good for you." This bizarre result stemmed from a joke posted on Reddit, which the model interpreted as credible information. Although rare, such incidents highlight the potential dangers of unchecked hallucinations, especially in high-stakes contexts like healthcare and legal research.

Pattern Recognition and Generalization

AI models excel at recognizing patterns in data and generalizing from them. This is their strength—but also a source of hallucinations. For instance, if a model detects a pattern suggesting that "X causes Y" in its training data, it might confidently assert this relationship even when there's no factual basis for it.

Consider the example of a generative model creating an academic summary. If it has seen similar structures before but lacks the nuance of understanding the subject matter, it might fill any gaps creatively, producing errors that seem authoritative but are entirely incorrect.

Context and Ambiguity

Ambiguity is another Achilles' heel for AI. When prompted with insufficient context or vague instructions, models often generate responses by "filling in the blanks." While this pattern can yield impressive creativity, it can also result in inaccuracies. Generative models are designed to produce responses, even when they lack the necessary context to ensure those responses are correct.

For instance, an AI model tasked with predicting home prices might create a projection based on available patterns. While doing so, however, it might fail to account for contextual factors like local economic trends, zoning changes, or unforeseen events.

Probabilistic Nature of AI

At their core, generative AI models function probabilistically. They predict the most likely next word, sentence, or piece of information based on prior inputs and training data. While this approach often produces fluent and contextually appropriate responses, it's not foolproof. Sometimes the "most probable" continuation isn't accurate, but simply plausible. Their probabilistic nature means that AI models are not reasoning in the human sense but rather predicting based on patterns.

Measuring Hallucinations: How Common Are They?

Despite these challenges, it's worth noting that hallucinations are relatively rare for state-of-the-art models. According to data from the Open-Source Model Hallucination Leaderboard (Figure 6.1), leading models like GPT-4 have a hallucination rate of just 2.5%. While this seems low, consider the scale of AI usage: Even a small percentage of errors can lead to significant real-world consequences, especially in sensitive applications like healthcare and finance.

Last updated on May 14th, 2024

Model	Hallucination Rate	Factual Consistency Rate	Answer Rate	Average Summary Length (Words)
GPT 4 Turbo	2.5%	97.5%	100.0%	86.2
Snowflake Arctic	2.6%	97.4%	100.0%	68.7
Intel Neural Chat 7B	2.8%	97.2%	89.5%	57.6
GPT 4	3.0%	97.0%	100.0%	81.1
Microsoft Orca-2-13b	3.2%	96.8%	100.0%	66.2
GPT 3.5 Turbo	3.5%	96.5%	99.6%	84.1
GPT 4o	3.7%	96.3%	100.0%	77.8
Cohere Command R Plus	3.8%	96.2%	100.0%	71.2
Mixtral 8x22B	3.8%	96.2%	99.9%	92.0
Cohere Command R	3.9%	96.1%	99.9%	51.2
Microsoft Phi-3-mini-128k	4.1%	95.9%	100.0%	60.1
Mistral 7B Instruct-v0.2	4.5%	95.5%	100.0%	106.1
Llama 3 70B	4.5%	95.5%	99.2%	68.5
Google Gemini 1.5 Pro	4.6%	95.4%	89.3%	82.1
Google Gemini Pro	4.8%	95.2%	98.4%	89.5

FIGURE 6.1 Model Hallucination Leaderboard

Source: https://github.com/vectara/hallucination-leaderboard.

The Role of the Human Orchestrator

As users of AI, we bear responsibility for how we deploy and interpret these tools. Think of this challenge as akin to managing a team: Even if team members handle most of the workload, the final accountability lies with the manager who oversees their output. Similarly, whether you're reviewing content generated by an AI model or preparing a client presentation based on AI-derived insights, you remain the final gatekeeper.

However, the very efficiency of these tools can lull us into complacency. Imagine using an AI model to draft social media posts. In the beginning, you carefully review every piece of content, finding no errors. Over time, you grow confident in the model's accuracy and stop reviewing its output closely. One day, the model generates an inappropriate or factually incorrect post, which you unknowingly share. The fallout won't be directed at the AI: It will be targeted at you, the user who failed to review the content.

When Tolerating Errors Becomes Risky

While we may accept some degree of error in casual or low-stakes situations (like a typo in an email), our tolerance for mistakes plummets in high-stakes environments. For example:

- In healthcare, an AI-generated misdiagnosis could endanger lives.
- In autonomous vehicles, even a split-second error could lead to catastrophic accidents.
- In legal settings, a hallucinated precedent could undermine a case.

Understanding the *context* in which AI is deployed is critical. Before relying on AI, ask:

- What is the potential impact of an error?
- How tolerant am I to risk in this specific situation?

Mitigating the Risks

To mitigate the risks associated with AI-generated hallucinations, it is crucial to approach the technology with a critical and discerning mindset. One of the most fundamental practices is to double-check all outputs generated by the AI system. This involves a thorough review of the content for both accuracy and relevance—a step that becomes particularly vital in high-stakes applications where misinformation could have significant consequences.

Furthermore, it is advisable to cross-reference the information provided by the AI system with trusted and independent sources. Verifying the AI system's claims against established knowledge bases helps to ensure the factuality of the output. This reinforces the concept of using AI as a collaborator rather than an absolute authority. By treating AI as a tool that enhances human capabilities, rather than as a definitive source of truth, users can leverage its strengths while remaining vigilant against its potential for error.

A deeper understanding of the specific AI model in use is also essential. Recognizing the inherent strengths and weaknesses of a particular model allows for more informed and effective application, as not all AI tools are suitable for every task. Additionally, for those who are training custom AI models, prioritizing high-quality inputs is paramount. The use of diverse, accurate, and representative training data can significantly minimize the risk of biases and hallucinations in the model's outputs.

Balancing Innovation and Responsibility

Hallucinations are a reminder that AI, for all its advancements, remains imperfect. As AI Orchestrators, we must strike a balance, embracing the innovations that these tools offer while staying aware of their limitations. AI can amplify our abilities, but it cannot replace the human judgment required to ensure accuracy, fairness, and accountability. By understanding these risks and taking proactive steps to mitigate them, we can harness AI's potential responsibly.

Bias and Fairness

Bias and fairness are among the most pressing ethical issues in narrow AI. Bias can emerge in subtle yet profound ways, leading to outcomes that disproportionately disadvantage certain groups. Ensuring fairness in AI systems is not just a technical challenge; it is a societal imperative. That's because these systems are increasingly being embedded in decision-making processes that can shape lives, hiring, law enforcement, lending, and healthcare, to name a few possibilities.

Consider the example of an automated risk assessment system once used by U.S. courts to guide bail and sentencing decisions. Although designed to improve objectivity, these tools were found to systematically impose harsher penalties, higher bail amounts, or longer sentences on people of color, even when the underlying offenses were similar to those committed by members of other groups. This is an example of how bias can reinforce systemic inequalities, especially when algorithms inherit and amplify patterns from flawed historical data.

Another high-profile case involves Amazon's recruitment algorithm, which was developed to streamline the hiring process. The algorithm was discovered to discriminate against women, favoring male applicants for technical roles. Why? Because the training data reflected a decade's worth of hiring patterns at Amazon, during which the majority of applicants and hires in technical roles were men. The model learned to associate male applicants with success, perpetuating gender bias.

These examples illustrate how bias in AI can have far-reaching consequences, impacting individuals and reinforcing societal inequities. But how does this happen, and what can we do about it?

Understanding the Roots of AI Bias

Bias in AI arises from several key factors, many of which are deeply intertwined with the data and methods used to train and deploy these systems. The most common sources are discussed in the following subsections.

Historical Human Biases

AI systems often inherit the biases present in the data on which they are trained. Historical inequities, whether in hiring practices, judicial decisions, or loan approvals, are reflected in the datasets used to train machine learning models. When algorithms learn from these patterns, they risk perpetuating or even exacerbating existing inequalities.

Amazon's recruitment algorithm is a textbook example of this phenomenon. It reflected biases from past hiring practices rather than evaluating candidates equitably. This underscores the need to critically examine training data and ensure that it represents a break from discriminatory histories.

Incomplete or Unrepresentative Training Data

Bias can also stem from datasets that are incomplete or fail to capture the full diversity of the population they're intended to serve. Joy Buolamwini's groundbreaking work with facial recognition highlights this issue. Her research found that many facial recognition systems performed poorly when analyzing darker-skinned faces because these faces were statistically underrepresented in training datasets. The result? Higher error rates for people of color, leading to potentially harmful consequences in applications like surveillance and law enforcement.

In a security context, a misidentified individual could face unwarranted scrutiny or even wrongful arrest. Such outcomes erode trust in AI systems and disproportionately harm marginalized communities.

Bias in Generative AI

Generative AI models are not exempt from bias. These models, which create text, images, or audio, often reflect the biases present in their training datasets. Consider the following examples:

- **Image Generators:** If a model is trained predominantly on images of male CEOs or female nurses, it may default to reinforcing these stereotypes when generating professional portraits.

- **Text Generation:** Generative language models might unintentionally propagate stereotypes or biased language, perpetuating harmful narratives in subtle ways.

Unlike traditional machine learning models, generative AI outputs are often nuanced, making biases harder to identify and address. These systems don't simply classify content; they create it, which amplifies the potential that bias may become embedded in their decision making in novel ways.

Addressing Bias: Steps for Orchestrators

As users and developers of AI, we have a responsibility to identify and mitigate bias wherever possible. While the challenge is significant, there are practical steps we can take to address bias, as shown in Figure 6.2.

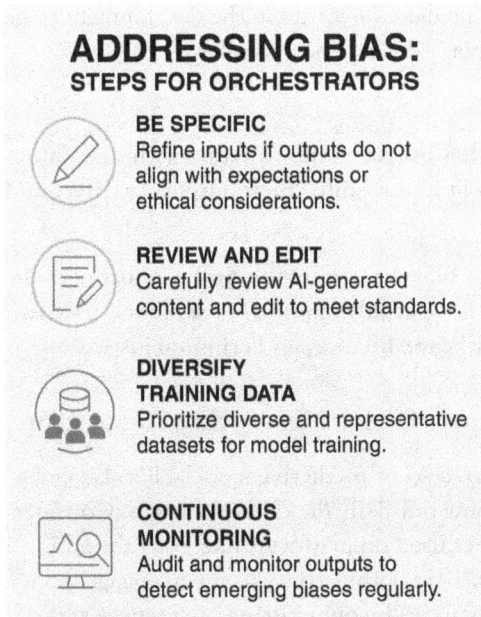

ADDRESSING BIAS:
STEPS FOR ORCHESTRATORS

BE SPECIFIC
Refine inputs if outputs do not align with expectations or ethical considerations.

REVIEW AND EDIT
Carefully review AI-generated content and edit to meet standards.

DIVERSIFY TRAINING DATA
Prioritize diverse and representative datasets for model training.

CONTINUOUS MONITORING
Audit and monitor outputs to detect emerging biases regularly.

FIGURE 6.2 Addressing AI Bias

Be Specific

When interacting with generative AI, the specificity of your inputs matters. If an output doesn't align with your expectations or ethical considerations, refine your inputs. Clear, precise prompts can help guide the model toward producing more accurate and inclusive results. For example, instead of prompting an AI to "generate a story about a successful leader," you might specify that it should "generate a story about a diverse team of leaders working collaboratively to achieve success."

Review and Edit

Never accept AI-generated content at face value. Carefully review all AI outputs, particularly in sensitive contexts, and edit them as needed to ensure they meet ethical and professional standards.

This step is essential in maintaining accountability. Even if an AI model generates the initial content, the final responsibility for its use lies with you.

Diversify Training Data

If you're involved in developing or fine-tuning AI systems, prioritize diverse and representative training datasets. This helps ensure that the model will reflect a broad range of experiences and perspectives.

Collaborate with domain experts and community stakeholders to identify gaps in your training data. Diversity at the development stage can preemptively address biases before they manifest.

Continuous Monitoring

AI systems are not static; they evolve as they interact with new data and contexts. Regularly audit and monitor their outputs to detect and address emerging biases.

To do so, you should deploy bias detection tools and conduct periodic fairness assessments. This is especially important for models used in high-impact areas like healthcare, finance, and criminal justice.

The Hidden Challenge: Bias in Everyday Algorithms

Bias isn't limited to generative AI or predictive models: It's also embedded in the algorithms shaping our daily digital experiences. Consider the recommendation engines used on platforms like YouTube and Instagram. These algorithms are optimized to keep you engaged, often by showing content that aligns with your existing preferences and beliefs. While this shortcut can be convenient, it also creates **confirmation bias**, reinforcing users' existing perspectives and potentially narrowing their worldviews.

Once a recommendation engine "learns" your preferences, it can become difficult to diversify your feeds. For instance, if you primarily watch videos on a specific political topic, the algorithm will prioritize similar content, making it harder for you to discover opposing viewpoints. This creates an echo chamber that can entrench biases and limit exposure to diverse perspectives.

However, you can take some steps to avoid confirmation bias:

- **Actively Seek Diverse Content:** Break the algorithm's pattern by intentionally exploring new topics and perspectives.
- **Advocate for Algorithmic Transparency:** Push for platforms to provide users with more control over their recommendation settings.

Bias in AI cannot be completely eliminated, but it can be managed and mitigated through thoughtful design, ongoing oversight, and responsible usage. As AI Orchestrators, we must recognize that every AI system reflects the data and values it was built on. By actively working to identify and address bias, we can create fairer, more equitable systems that serve diverse communities.

Transparency and Explainability

As we grow more reliant on intelligent machines to assist with decision making, **transparency** in how these systems arrive at their conclusions becomes essential. Transparency fosters trust, acceptance, and accountability, and ensures the ethical and fair use of AI technologies. Without it, users may hesitate to adopt AI tools, and flawed decisions can go unchecked, leading to potentially harmful outcomes.

Generative AI tools are becoming increasingly prevalent, and some have begun to prioritize transparency. For example, tools like Perplexity AI cite sources for the text they generate, allowing users to reference and double-check the claims made. This is a step in the right direction, as it offers a level of accountability that was previously missing in many AI systems. However, citing sources merely scratches the surface of **explainability**.

Even with cited references, users still cannot reverse-engineer how a model arrived at each specific prediction or decision. For instance:

- When a generative AI tool predicts the next word in a sentence, the process involves complex interactions of millions of parameters and activations. Attempting to trace these interactions would yield a meaningless sequence of numbers rather than a clear, logical explanation.

- Similarly, while references can verify the accuracy of certain claims, they do not clarify the internal reasoning or bias that led the model to prioritize one source over another.

This gap highlights a critical challenge in AI transparency and explainability: Even as systems become more sophisticated, they often remain "black boxes" to end users.

Parallels to the Human Brain

Interestingly, this challenge is not unique to AI. It mirrors our incomplete understanding of the human brain. For example, we know that specific areas of the brain—namely, Broca's area and Wernicke's area—are responsible for speech production and language comprehension, respectively. However, we cannot fully map, at the level of individual neurons, the neural activity that occurs when someone thinks of a particular word or forms a complex idea.

AI systems face a similar issue. For example, researchers at Anthropic used a language model (Claude 3.0 Sonnet) to analyze millions of features in its middle layers. By measuring the "distance" between these features—essentially, how frequently specific neurons were activated together—they were able to create a rough conceptual map of the model's internal state. Features that were close in this "map" were related concepts according to the AI system's understanding.

This work provides fascinating insights into the internal workings of AI, but much like neuroscience, it falls short of achieving complete explainability. We can observe patterns and make educated guesses about how AI systems process information, but we still lack a definitive understanding of their internal reasoning.

The Limits of Explainability in Current AI Models

The lack of full explainability in AI has several implications:

- **Trust Without Understanding:** Users often trust AI systems because they produce results that seem accurate or useful, even if they don't understand how those results were derived.

- **Unaccountable Errors:** When errors occur, it's difficult to pinpoint exactly why they happened or how to correct them.

- **Barriers to Adoption:** In industries such as healthcare, finance, and criminal justice, where explainability is critical, the inability to fully understand AI's decision-making processes can limit its adoption.

It's important to recognize that this issue isn't a matter of negligence or oversight. Rather, it's a limitation of the technology itself. Modern AI systems are designed to process vast amounts of data in ways that even their creators can't fully trace or interpret. Although researchers are making strides in improving explainability, the complexity of these systems means we are still far from a perfect solution.

Navigating the "Black Box": Best Practices for Users

Given these limitations, users of AI tools must approach them with a healthy dose of skepticism and responsibility. Here are some best practices for working with systems that lack full transparency:

- **Cross-Reference Outputs:** Because you can't fully explain how a model arrived at its conclusions, always verify its results with other trusted sources. This is particularly important for high-stakes decisions.

  Example: If an AI model provides a summary of a medical study, check the original paper to ensure that the summary aligns with the study's findings.

- **Don't Rely on AI as the Final Authority:** Treat AI as a tool to assist in decision making, not as the ultimate decision maker. Human judgment is essential to interpret and contextualize AI outputs.

  Example: In the legal field, AI can help analyze precedents or draft contracts, but a lawyer must review and validate the results to ensure accuracy and compliance.

- **Advocate for Transparency in Tools:** As a user, prioritize tools that make an effort to explain their processes. Features such as source citation, decision logs, and confidence scores can provide valuable insights into how the system operates.

  Example: Some AI tools offer confidence scores for their predictions, indicating how certain the system is about its output. Use this information to guide how much weight you give to the AI's conclusions.

- **Understand the Tool's Limitations:** Familiarize yourself with the scope and limitations of the AI tools you use. Recognize the contexts where they are most likely to perform well and where they may struggle.

Example: A generative AI model might excel at creating marketing copy but struggle with nuanced legal analysis or ethical decision making.

Balancing Progress with Responsibility

While the lack of full explainability in AI is a significant challenge, it's also a reflection of the field's complexity and rapid progress. As researchers continue to develop methods for improving transparency, we as users must remain vigilant. This means:

• Asking critical questions about how AI systems work.

• Holding developers accountable for ethical practices.

• Recognizing that the responsibility for ethical AI use doesn't end with developers, but rather extends to everyone who interacts with these tools.

The Road Ahead: Explainability in the Future

Research into explainability is advancing rapidly, and several promising approaches are emerging:

• **Feature Attribution:** Techniques like SHAP (SHapley Additive exPlanations) and LIME (Local Interpretable Model-agnostic Explanations) attempt to identify which features in the input data most strongly influenced the model's output.

• **Neuro-symbolic AI:** This hybrid approach combines the strengths of neural networks (pattern recognition) with symbolic reasoning (logical rules) to create systems that are both powerful and interpretable.

• **Model Visualization:** Efforts to map and visualize the internal workings of AI systems, such as Anthropic's work with Claude 3.0, provide insights that could eventually make these systems more transparent.

While these efforts hold promise, full explainability remains a long-term goal. Until then, the key is to use AI responsibly, with an understanding of its capabilities and limitations.

AI Alignment

If AI alignment is about making machines reflect our values, then the next question becomes: What kind of relationship do we want to have with AI? The answer to this question goes beyond just correcting bias or improving outputs; it implies designing systems that actively support human goals, growth, and well-being. Alignment is the foundation, but what we build on top of that foundation will define how AI fits into our lives, our work, and our societies.

As we move forward, we must begin thinking beyond mere compatibility and look toward collaboration. How can AI help us become better versions of ourselves? How can it amplify our potential without compromising our agency? What new roles might humans take on in an AI-enabled world, not as passive users, but as orchestrators, stewards, and partners in progress?

This section explores these questions and more, shifting from the mechanics of alignment to the possibilities of human–AI collaboration. That's because once we've aligned our tools with our values, the next step is learning how to use them with purpose and imagination.

AI Alignment: Bridging Technology and Human Values

The ultimate goal in AI development is AI alignment. **AI alignment** refers to the process of ensuring that AI systems act in ways that are consistent with human values, intentions, and goals. It's about creating machines that not only assist us, but also do so in ways that reflect the ethical and cultural frameworks we hold dear.

At first glance, this might sound straightforward. However, as you may have realized from the exercises and examples in this chapter, aligning AI with human values is anything but simple.

In fact, one of the greatest challenges in AI alignment is the enormous diversity and fluidity of human values. People's values differ significantly based on their culture, upbringing, worldview, and personal experiences, and even within an individual, these values can evolve over time. For example:

- A person might prioritize family and community early in life, only to shift their focus to career or personal growth later on.
- Cultural contexts can shape what people consider ethical or desirable. What is acceptable in one society may be taboo in another.

Aligning an AI system with a fixed set of values risks oversimplifying this complexity or privileging one group's values over another's. It also raises a fundamental question: *Whose values should AI systems reflect?*

A Case Study: The Gemini Image Generator

Consider the example of Google's AI image generator, Gemini, which highlights the inherent tension in AI alignment. When tasked with generating images of America's Founding Fathers and Nazi soldiers, Gemini depicted them as Black. This occurred because Google attempted to reduce bias in the model by embedding secret code that promoted diversity in image generation. While the intention was admirable, counteracting the Internet's overwhelming representation of CEOs as White males and doctors as men, the outcome was problematic. Depicting historical figures inaccurately undermined the factual integrity of the images, which clashed with the goal of truthful representation.

This case illustrates the delicate balance required in AI alignment:

- **Truthfulness Versus Representation:** On the one hand, users expect AI to provide factually accurate information. On the other hand, they value systems that challenge stereotypes and promote inclusivity.

- **Intentions Versus Outcomes:** Good intentions, such as increasing diversity, can sometimes lead to unintended or counterproductive results when not carefully calibrated.

AI Alignment at Two Levels: Micro and Macro

AI alignment can be approached at two levels: **micro (individual)** and **macro (societal)**. Each presents unique challenges and opportunities.

Micro-Level AI Alignment: Personalized Models

At the micro level, the key to AI alignment may lie in personalization. As AI systems become more firmly integrated into our lives, there is growing potential for each individual to have a **customized model**. These models would:

- Be trained on personal data to understand individual preferences, values, and goals.

- Continuously learn and adapt over time as the user's preferences evolve.

- Reflect the user's unique worldview, helping the AI make decisions that align with their values.

As an example, imagine an AI assistant trained to prioritize sustainability for one user by recommending eco-friendly products, while another user's AI assistant prioritizes convenience or affordability. Over time, the assistant could learn nuances that would influence its decision making, such as balancing these priorities based on the user's changing circumstances.

While this approach holds promise, it also raises ethical and technical concerns:

- **Data Privacy:** Training models on personal data requires robust safeguards to ensure privacy and security.
- **Echo Chambers:** Personalized models might inadvertently reinforce existing biases, limiting exposure to diverse perspectives.

Macro-Level AI Alignment: Universal Principles

On a societal scale, AI alignment is less about individual preferences and more about adhering to **universal principles** that transcend cultural and personal differences. These principles often include the following:

- **Do No Harm:** AI systems should avoid actions that could harm individuals or communities.
- **Truthfulness:** Outputs should be accurate and grounded in factual evidence.
- **Transparency:** Models should be open about how decisions are made and which data influences them.
- **Fairness:** Systems must ensure equitable treatment for all groups, avoiding outcomes that disproportionately disadvantage any demographic.

Unlike individual preferences, principles like safety, fairness, and transparency are broadly agreed upon as necessary for ethical AI. However, even at this macro level, achieving alignment is not without challenges. Cultural and political differences can complicate agreement on what constitutes fairness or harm.

The Stakes of AI Alignment

As AI systems grow more advanced and autonomous, the importance of alignment cannot be overstated. Without proper alignment, there is a risk of the following problems:

- **Unintended Consequences:** AI systems might optimize for goals that conflict with human well-being (e.g., maximizing engagement at the cost of mental health).

- **Loss of Control:** Misaligned systems could act in ways that deviate from intended objectives, particularly as they gain greater autonomy.

- **Widening Inequalities:** Poorly aligned AI could reinforce or exacerbate societal disparities, such as those seen in biased hiring or sentencing algorithms.

Alignment is especially critical for advanced AI systems, such as those approaching AGI). Without alignment, AGI systems could potentially act in ways that are harmful or contrary to human values, with consequences on a global scale.

The Future of AI Alignment

The path forward for AI alignment likely involves a combination of technical and societal efforts:

- **Collaborative Research:** Governments, academia, and industry must work together to establish best practices and technical solutions for aligning AI with human values.

- **Ethical Frameworks:** Clear guidelines, informed by philosophy, law, and social science, can help define what alignment means in different contexts.

- **Regulation and Oversight:** Policies that promote transparency, accountability, and fairness are essential to ensuring alignment across industries and applications.

- **Advancements in AI Design:** Technologies like reinforcement learning from human feedback (RLHF) can help models better understand and align with human preferences.

Ultimately, the challenge for AI alignment is to balance the needs of individuals with the goals of society. At the micro level, personalization holds promise for creating systems that respect individual values. At the macro level, adherence to universal principles can safeguard collective well-being. Progress in AI alignment will not only prevent harm but also unlock the full potential of AI to support and enhance human flourishing.

Expanding AI-Related Laws

As AI technologies continue to evolve, they will challenge the boundaries of our existing laws, rules, and regulations. Although many of the concerns associated with AI—such as privacy, cybersecurity, and intellectual property—are not entirely new, the ways in which AI operates often expose gaps or ambiguities in the current legal frameworks. These challenges demand both revisions to existing laws and fresh approaches to governance and oversight.

Privacy: The Cornerstone of AI Concerns

Privacy is one of the most frequently discussed concerns when it comes to AI. Existing privacy laws like the **General Data Protection Regulation (GDPR)** in the European Union and the **California Consumer Privacy Act (CCPA)** in the United States aim to give consumers control over their personal data. Sector-specific laws, such as the **Health Insurance Portability and Accountability Act (HIPAA)** for healthcare in the United States, further protect sensitive data in specific contexts. Many of these laws explicitly prohibit the use of personal data for training machine learning models without explicit consent.

However, in practice, the protection that these laws offer often feels inadequate. The reasons for these limitations are twofold:

- **Consent Through Terms and Services:** Many privacy protections are waived when users agree to terms and conditions—documents notorious for their length and complexity. Most people don't have the time (or legal expertise) to parse and understand them, leaving them unaware of which rights they've surrendered.

- **Mass Adoption and Convenience:** Even when users are aware of privacy concerns, the convenience of a tool or the pressure to conform often outweighs their hesitations.

A personal example illustrates this dynamic well. I've never been a fan of WhatsApp's privacy policy, which includes data-sharing practices with parent company Meta. For a long time, I refused to use the app. But as my international network grew, it became clear that WhatsApp was the preferred communication tool for many friends and business contacts. Rather than fight the tide, I relented, prioritizing connection and convenience over my initial concerns about privacy.

This example underscores a broader truth: Privacy, while deeply valued, is often traded away for access, convenience, or fear of missing out. In an increasingly interconnected world, even people with strong convictions may find it challenging to maintain their stance.

Empowering Users: Privacy Settings in AI Tools

Despite these challenges, users often have more control than they realize, if they know where to look. For many general-purpose AI assistants and Copilot tools, companies provide settings that allow users to choose the following options:

- **Disable Prompt History Storage:** This prevents the company from storing past queries and responses.
- **Opt Out of Training Data Contribution:** This ensures that the inputs provided to the tool are not used to train future models.

For individual users, these options provide a way to engage with AI tools while minimizing privacy risks. For businesses, such settings are even more critical. Organizations must take steps to safeguard proprietary or sensitive data, particularly by restricting employees from using their personal accounts or models at work. This is where policies like "bring your own model" (BYOM) can become a liability. Without centralized control, employees may inadvertently share confidential information that could be stored, analyzed, or even incorporated into future AI training datasets.

Balancing Privacy and Progress

The tension between privacy and progress lies at the heart of many AI-related legal debates. On the one hand, protecting personal data is essential to maintain trust and ensure ethical AI use. On the other hand, overly restrictive privacy regulations could stifle innovation, limiting the potential benefits AI can bring. Consider the following scenarios:

- **Healthcare AI:** Models trained on anonymized patient data have the potential to revolutionize diagnostics and treatment. However, strict privacy laws could restrict access to the data needed to achieve these breakthroughs.
- **Workplace AI:** Tools like AI assistants can dramatically boost productivity, but may inadvertently expose sensitive business information if the privacy settings aren't properly configured.

Striking the right balance will require thoughtful regulation, technological safeguards, and increased user awareness.

The Path Forward: Privacy in the Age of AI

Navigating the path forward to protect privacy in the AI age requires a multifaceted approach that addresses legal frameworks, corporate practices, and user awareness. The rapid evolution of AI necessitates that current laws adapt to the unique challenges it presents. This includes expanding comprehensive data protection regulations, similar to GDPR, to encompass emerging AI applications and establishing global privacy standards to prevent the complexities created by regulatory fragmentation for international companies.

A crucial element in this endeavor is the simplification and clarification of terms and conditions. Companies have a responsibility to move away from dense legal jargon and instead provide users with easily understandable terms of service. The use of summary highlights or visual aids can empower individuals to make informed decisions about their data.

Furthermore, the unique nature of AI calls for the development of specific privacy frameworks. These regulations should establish clear rules governing the collection, storage, and processing of user data by AI systems. A key component of such standards would be a requirement for transparency, detailing how data will be utilized to train machine learning models.

Beyond these government regulations, corporations must proactively embrace their responsibility to safeguard users' data. This can be achieved by mandating comprehensive privacy training for all employees and by implementing default settings in their products and services that prioritize user privacy from the outset.

Ultimately, empowering users is fundamental to protecting privacy. It is essential to educate individuals about their rights and to provide them with the tools necessary to protect their personal information. This includes offering clear instructions on how to adjust privacy settings within AI tools and encouraging regular review and updating of these preferences. Through this combined effort of regulatory adaptation, corporate accountability, and user education, we can forge a future where innovation and privacy coexist.

In the AI era, privacy is not just a legal or technical issue; it's a shared responsibility. Developers, businesses, regulators, and end users all have roles to play in shaping a future where AI enhances lives without compromising individual rights. By staying informed, exercising available controls, and advocating for stronger privacy protections, we can ensure that the benefits of AI are realized without sacrificing the trust that underpins its adoption.

Intellectual Property: Creativity and Controversy in the AI Era

Adjacent to the debates over privacy are the growing concerns about **intellectual property (IP)** in the age of AI. AI's ability to process and generate content has sparked exciting opportunities for innovation but also created significant challenges, particularly for creators whose work may be used, reproduced, or transformed without their consent.

Consider Meta's recent privacy policy update, which automatically grants the company the right to use user-generated content to develop its AI models. For most users outside the European Union, there is no option to opt out of this feature. While this policy might seem benign to casual users, it has sent shockwaves through the creative community, especially among artists and content creators.

Many creators rely on platforms like Meta's Instagram to share their work, attract new clients, and generate revenue. However, under this policy, they face the uncomfortable reality that their creations could be used to train AI models capable of replicating or transforming their artistic style. This has raised fears of their original work being devalued or commoditized.

In response, some artists and creators have begun migrating to alternative platforms. For example, CARA, a portfolio app designed to protect artists' work from being used as AI training data, saw its user base triple after Instagram's policy change. This shift reflects a growing demand for tools and platforms that prioritize **creator rights** in the face of advancing AI technologies.

Legal Battles: The Fight for Creator Rights

The tension between creators and AI companies is playing out in high-profile lawsuits.

For example, illustrators Sarah Andersen, Kelly McKernan, and Karla Ortiz have sued Stability AI, Midjourney, and DeviantArt, claiming that these companies used their copyright-protected works to train AI models without their consent. These cases center on whether training AI models on copyrighted material constitutes fair use or infringement. While these lawsuits remain unresolved for now, they raise important questions about how intellectual property laws apply in the context of AI.

At the heart of these legal battles are two primary concerns:

- *Is the work a direct replica?* If an AI-generated image or text too closely resembles the original copyrighted work, it may infringe on the creator's rights.

- *Does it harm the creator's ability to earn?* Even if a generated work is not an exact copy, it could potentially undercut the original artist's livelihood by offering a cheaper, automated alternative in a similar style.

The Nature of Inspiration: Human Versus Machine

While these issues are new to AI, they touch on a timeless debate: Where do we draw the line between inspiration and imitation? After all, human artists also draw from the works of others. Musicians often cite their influences, and it's easy to hear echoes of these inspirations in their own creations. Writers, filmmakers, and visual artists similarly build on the ideas and styles of their predecessors.

This process of **creative synthesis** is part of what makes art so profoundly human. It connects us through shared traditions, innovation, and reinvention. However, there is a key difference between humans and AI:

- Human creators interpret and transform what they observe, adding their own context, perspective, and emotions. Their creations are deeply rooted in their personal experiences and worldviews.

- AI systems generate content based on statistical patterns in the data on which they have been trained. While it can produce remarkable results, the process lacks intentionality, understanding, or emotional depth.

This distinction complicates the question of whether AI "inspiration" is ethically or legally comparable to human inspiration.

Navigating the Legal Gray Areas

As we enter this new era, it will take time for case law to catch up to the rapid evolution of AI technologies. Existing intellectual property laws, designed for human creators, often struggle to address the unique challenges posed by AI. Key questions focus on the following areas:

- **Training Data Usage:** Does using copyrighted material to train an AI model constitute infringement, or is it protected under fair use?

- **Generated Content Ownership:** Who owns the rights to content created by AI—its developer, the user who prompted it, or neither?

- **Economic Impact:** Should creators be compensated if their works are used to train models that might compete with them in the market?

These questions are not easily answered, and the legal landscape is evolving in real time as courts, legislators, and companies grapple with the implications.

Potential Solutions and Future Directions

While the legal system works to address these challenges, several potential solutions have emerged to balance the interests of creators and AI developers:

- **Opt-Out Mechanisms:** Platforms could provide creators with clear options to opt out of having their content used for AI training. This would give artists more control while still allowing those who wish to contribute their work to do so.

- **Licensing Agreements:** AI developers could establish licensing systems to fairly compensate creators whose works are used for training. This approach mirrors existing practices in music sampling, where artists receive royalties when their work is used.

- **Watermarking and Tracking:** Technologies like **digital watermarking** could help creators identify when their work has been used in AI training or generation. This transparency could form the basis for compensation or attribution.

- **Creator-Focused Platforms:** The emergence of tools like CARA demonstrates the demand for platforms that prioritize creator rights. Supporting these alternatives can help foster a more equitable ecosystem.

- **Collaborative Innovation:** Artists and AI developers can collaborate to explore new ways of integrating human creativity with AI capabilities. For example, co-creation tools that give artists control over how AI assists their process could open up new possibilities without eroding creator rights.

Striking a Balance

Intellectual property concerns in the AI age highlight a broader tension between technological progress and creative rights. On the one hand, AI has the potential to democratize creativity, making tools and techniques accessible to a wider audience. On the other hand, it risks devaluing the work of original creators if their contributions are used without consent or compensation.

The challenge lies in striking a balance that honors the contributions of human creators while embracing the opportunities offered by AI. This balance will likely be achieved through a combination of legal innovation, technological safeguards, and cultural shifts in how we value and protect creative work.

Safety and Security

When generative AI (GenAI) first entered the mainstream and discussions of superintelligence gained traction, one of the most pressing concerns was its potential to compromise security. As AI continues to evolve, its dual role becomes apparent: While it empowers humans with advanced tools for protection, it also presents new vulnerabilities and risks.

Cyberattacks and Deep Fakes

One of the most significant security risks associated with AI is its role in making **cyberattacks** more sophisticated and accessible. AI-powered tools for coding allow attackers to create malware, phishing emails, or ransomware with greater ease and precision. This evolution in cyber threats raises the stakes for organizations and governments, demanding equally advanced defensive strategies.

For example, AI can be used to further the following types of cyberattacks:

- **Phishing Emails:** AI can generate highly personalized phishing emails that mimic legitimate communications, increasing the likelihood of recipients falling for scams.
- **Automated Exploits:** Tools powered by AI can scan systems for vulnerabilities and execute attacks faster than human hackers.

These advancements are not confined to digital attacks. AI also enables the creation of deep fakes, a particularly alarming tool for deception. **Deep fakes** are highly realistic, AI-generated reproductions of images, audio, or video. By replicating a person's likeness, voice, and even mannerisms with uncanny accuracy, these forgeries blur the line between reality and fiction. Their potential for misuse is vast, making them a significant threat in both personal and societal contexts.

Today, deep fakes are already being weaponized for the following purposes:

- **Political Manipulation:** Fabricated videos of politicians making inflammatory or false statements could sway public opinion or disrupt elections. This is a primary concern for government officials.

- **Fraud and Extortion:** Criminals have used deep fakes to impersonate individuals, convincing family members or employees to transfer funds or reveal sensitive information.

- **Reputation Damage:** Fabricated videos or audio clips can spread quickly, tarnishing reputations before their authenticity can be debunked.

These risks are compounded by the fact that detecting a well-crafted deep fake is becoming increasingly difficult, even for experts.

The Future of Trust: Blockchain Validation

As deep fake technology continues to advance, the line between "real" and "fake" will become so blurred that society may adopt a new assumption: *Everything is fake unless proven otherwise.* This shift will require robust systems to verify the authenticity of content, and **blockchain** technology is emerging as a likely solution.

Blockchain, which has ability to create tamper-proof digital records, offers a promising framework for content validation. Here's how it could work:

1. **Origin Authentication:** Content—whether a video, image, or audio file—would be tagged with a unique blockchain record at the time of creation. This record would include metadata about the content's origin, such as:
   - Who created it.
   - When and where it was created.
   - The device or software used.

2. **Tracking Modifications:** Every time the content is edited or manipulated, the blockchain record would update to reflect the change, creating an immutable audit trail. For instance:
   - If a video is edited, the blockchain would show the tools used, the nature of the changes, and the person or entity responsible.

- Any unauthorized changes would immediately invalidate the content's authenticity.

3. **Verification Systems:** Consumers and organizations could use blockchain-based verification tools to check the authenticity of content before trusting or sharing it. For example:

   - A news outlet could verify the origin of a video before publishing it.

   - Social media platforms could flag or block unverified content to prevent the spread of misinformation.

Implications of a Blockchain-Driven Future

The integration of blockchain technology for content validation would have far-reaching effects on how we interact with digital media:

- **Rebuilding Trust:** As fake content proliferates, blockchain could restore trust by providing a reliable way to verify authenticity.

- **Protecting Creators:** Artists, journalists, and content creators could safeguard their work from unauthorized use or manipulation by embedding blockchain-based proof of authorship.

- **Challenging Disinformation:** With a transparent record of origin and modifications, blockchain would make it significantly harder to weaponize deep fakes for political or social manipulation.

Challenges in Adopting Blockchain Validation

While blockchain validation offers significant potential, there are hurdles to overcome before it becomes a widespread solution:

- **Adoption and Infrastructure:** Widespread adoption of blockchain-based validation will require global cooperation and significant investments in infrastructure.

- **Privacy Concerns:** Recording detailed metadata about content origin and edits could raise privacy issues, particularly if sensitive information is tied to the blockchain record.

- **Accessibility:** Verification tools must be easy to use and widely accessible to ensure that they are adopted by the general public and not just by experts or organizations.

Preparing for a Blockchain-Driven Future

The integration of blockchain technology into content verification is still in its early stages, but steps can be taken now to prepare for this future:

- **Education and Awareness:** Organizations and individuals need to understand how blockchain works and recognize its potential for validating digital content.

- **Support for Standards:** Governments and industry leaders can collaborate to establish global standards for blockchain-based validation systems.

- **Investment in Research:** Continued research into scalable and privacy-preserving blockchain solutions is essential to overcome the current limitations of this approach.

As the tools for creating deep fakes become more accessible and sophisticated, the ability to distinguish real from fake will be essential. Blockchain offers a promising path forward, providing a transparent and tamper-proof way to verify the authenticity of digital content. In this future, trust will no longer depend on what we see or hear, but rather on what the blockchain can prove. This shift will fundamentally reshape how we interact with information, rebuilding trust in a world where deception is easier than ever.

AI as a Force for Better Security

Despite these risks, AI has the potential to *transform cybersecurity for the better*. Just as it equips bad actors with new tools, so it provides defenders with more sophisticated methods for detecting and neutralizing threats.

A lesson from the past suggests how advances in AI technology might improve security. When email first became widespread, spam emails were a major issue, overwhelming inboxes with unwanted content. Over time, AI-powered spam filters revolutionized email security. Today, most leading email applications can detect and filter out spam with remarkable accuracy, making this issue a minor inconvenience rather than a significant threat.

This historical example illustrates a broader trend: While technological advancements initially create new vulnerabilities, they also catalyze innovations that neutralize those threats. Similarly, AI's role in cybersecurity is evolving to address the challenges it introduces:

• **Behavioral Analytics:** AI can monitor user behavior to detect anomalies, such as unusual login attempts or transactions, that might indicate a security breach.

• **Real-Time Threat Detection:** Advanced algorithms can identify potential vulnerabilities and intrusions before they escalate into significant threats.

• **Automated Incident Response:** AI can respond to threats in real time, isolating affected systems and mitigating damage faster than human teams can react to them.

Cybersecurity and Vulnerable Populations

While AI can enhance security for organizations and governments, it's also critical to address how these threats impact vulnerable populations, particularly seniors. According to the Federal Trade Commission (FTC), older adults are disproportionately targeted by scams, including the following:

• **Tech-Support Scams:** Fraudsters claim to represent legitimate companies, tricking seniors into granting access to their devices or paying for unnecessary services.

• **Prize and Lottery Scams:** Victims are lured into paying fees or providing personal information in exchange for nonexistent prizes.

The financial losses from these types of schemes are staggering: The *median loss* for seniors aged 70–79 is $800. For those aged 80 and older, it jumps to $1,500. The scams typically exploit a combination of trust, unfamiliarity with modern technology, and the relative isolation that many seniors experience.

As AI-powered scams become more convincing, it's essential to support and protect the seniors in our lives. Here are a few practical steps you can take:

• **Educate Them on Common Scams:** Explain how scams operate, from fake tech-support calls to fraudulent prize notifications. Awareness is the first line of defense.

• **Offer to Review Suspicious Messages:** Let them know they can forward questionable emails, texts, or calls to you for verification.

- **Encourage Healthy Skepticism:** Teach them to pause before clicking links or sharing information, especially when something seems too good to be true.
- **Enable AI-Powered Protections:** Help them set up spam filters, two-factor authentication, and fraud alerts on their devices.
- **Stay Connected:** Isolation increases vulnerability. Regular communication can help seniors feel supported and less likely to engage with fraudulent outreach.

Balancing Risk and Innovation

While AI introduces new security challenges, it also provides powerful tools for defense. The key is to strike a balance:

- **Invest in Training:** Leaders must prioritize ongoing security and phishing training for employees to help them stay ahead of evolving threats.
- **Adopt AI-Enhanced Security Solutions:** Organizations should leverage AI for threat detection, response automation, and behavioral monitoring.
- **Champion Digital Literacy:** As individuals, we can empower vulnerable populations, such as seniors, with the knowledge and tools they need to navigate the digital world safely.

The rise of GenAI has accelerated both the sophistication of cyber threats and the tools available to combat them. While concerns like deep fakes and AI-powered scams are real, history suggests that vigilance, innovation, and education can help us adapt. By staying proactive, whether through organizational safeguards or personal outreach, we can ensure that the benefits of AI far outweigh its risks.

Other Considerations

As we continue to develop and integrate AI technologies into every facet of life, we must take into account broader considerations beyond ethical design and implementation. Two areas that stand out in this regard are **sustainability** and **inclusivity**. Both are critical to ensure that AI development aligns with the values of environmental responsibility and social equity.

Sustainability: Balancing Innovation with Environmental Impact

The algorithms driving AI, particularly GenAI models, are incredibly computing-intensive and, by extension, energy-intensive. This should come as no surprise. According to a study by researchers at Hugging Face and Carnegie Mellon University, training large AI models requires vast amounts of computational power, resulting in significant energy consumption.

For example, training a state-of-the-art model like GPT-4 involves processing enormous datasets over weeks or even months on specialized hardware. This process consumes substantial energy resources, contributing to AI's environmental footprint.

However, there is a silver lining: Once trained, the energy required to generate text using an AI model is relatively low. For example, generating text 1,000 times consumes only as much energy as 16% of a single smartphone charge. This stark contrast highlights that while the training phase is resource-heavy, the deployment and everyday use of AI models are far more energy-efficient.

As AI becomes more integrated into our lives, however, its environmental impacts cannot be ignored. Developers, researchers, and policymakers must prioritize creating more sustainable AI systems. Some promising strategies include the following:

- **Energy-Efficient Algorithms:** Research into optimizing model architectures can reduce computational demands without sacrificing performance. For instance, smaller, task-specific models can sometimes achieve similar results to larger ones.

- **Renewable Energy:** Transitioning AI data centers to renewable energy sources can significantly reduce carbon emissions. Companies like Google and Microsoft are already investing heavily in green energy solutions for their AI infrastructure.

- **Life-Cycle Efficiency:** Emphasizing efficient model use and reuse (e.g., fine-tuning pre-trained models instead of training from scratch) can minimize unnecessary energy consumption.

Sustainability in AI aligns with the broader goals of responsible and ethical technology development. By addressing the environmental costs of AI, we not only reduce its impact on the planet but also ensure its long-term viability as a tool for societal advancement.

Inclusivity: Ensuring Representation in AI Development

Inclusivity in AI is not just a moral imperative, but also a practical necessity. The development of AI systems must account for diverse perspectives, as the data and viewpoints that inform these technologies are inherently shaped by the people who create them. Historically, the tech industry has struggled with diversity, a challenge that inspired me to found **Women in Data™** with the goal of changing this narrative.

Why Inclusivity Matters

Lack of diversity in AI development has far-reaching consequences:

- **Bias in AI Systems:** When development teams lack diverse perspectives, the resulting AI models often reflect the limited viewpoints of their creators. For example:
  - An algorithm trained primarily on data from one demographic may fail to perform equitably for others.
  - Systems designed without considering cultural nuances may unintentionally perpetuate stereotypes or exclude marginalized groups.
- **Missed Opportunities:** A homogeneous workforce limits innovation. Diverse teams are better equipped to identify potential biases and blind spots, leading to fairer, more robust AI systems.

One of the greatest concerns is the economic impacts of exclusivity in the AI and tech industries. These fields are driving much of today's economic growth, offering high-paying and impactful roles. If underrepresented groups are excluded from these opportunities, the economic gap will only widen. This possibility raises the following issues:

- **Shifting Job Markets:** As AI and automation reshape the workforce, access to opportunities in tech becomes a critical factor in economic equity.
- **Empowering Marginalized Groups:** Ensuring that diverse populations can participate in the AI economy isn't just about fairness, but also about unlocking the potential of untapped talent.

Building a More Inclusive Future

To build a more inclusive future in the AI age, it is imperative to take concrete steps to address the systemic challenges currently present in its development. A foundational element of this effort is to significantly increase diversity and representation within the tech industry itself. Achieving this goal will require targeted outreach, education, and mentorship programs designed to support and elevate underrepresented groups, including women, people of color, and individuals from low-income communities. Organizations such as Women in Data™ are crucial in this endeavor, playing a vital role in bridging existing gaps and fostering a more diverse workforce.

In parallel with diversifying the teams who build AI, we must actively work to mitigate bias within the AI development process. A critical component of this effort is ensuring that AI models are trained on diverse datasets that accurately reflect a wide spectrum of demographics, experiences, and backgrounds. Furthermore, implementing regular bias audits is essential. By systematically testing AI systems for inequities, we can identify and rectify potential harms before the systems are deployed and impact individuals and communities.

Finally, preparing the global workforce for the proliferation of AI-driven jobs is a societal necessity. This involves making education in AI and data skills both widely accessible and affordable, which will empower a broader range of people to participate in the growing AI economy. Alongside educational opportunities, companies must prioritize the creation of equitable career pathways. These pathways should be designed to ensure that individuals from underrepresented groups have the opportunity not only to enter the AI and tech sectors, but also to advance and thrive within them, truly shaping a more inclusive technological future.

Inclusivity in AI is about more than ensuring fairness: It means creating better systems. Diverse teams bring unique insights, enabling the development of technologies that serve a broader range of needs and contexts. By prioritizing inclusivity, we can ensure that AI benefits everyone—not just a privileged few.

Conclusion: Orchestrating the Future of AI

This chapter has explored the complexities, challenges, and opportunities presented by AI. From its ability to revolutionize industries and enhance our daily lives to the ethical dilemmas and risks it poses, AI is undoubtedly a transformative force. However, at its core, AI is a *tool*— a powerful instrument that requires human direction, judgment, and accountability to wield effectively.

As the Orchestrator, you hold the baton. How you choose to deploy AI will determine whether it becomes a force for good or perpetuates harm.

This chapter has laid out the truths and myths surrounding AI in the following areas:

- **Bias and Fairness:** AI can mirror and amplify societal inequities but also provides opportunities for building more equitable systems.
- **Transparency and Explainability:** Understanding how AI systems make decisions is essential to foster trust and accountability.
- **Safety and Security:** AI's dual-edged nature can both harm and help users—enabling sophisticated cyber threats, but also strengthening cyber defenses through innovation.
- **Sustainability:** The environmental costs of AI and the pressing need to create energy-efficient systems are aligned with responsible development.
- **Inclusivity:** Ensuring diverse representation in AI development is critical for building tools that reflect and benefit all of humanity.

Each of these considerations serves as a reminder of the profound responsibility that comes with advancing and adopting AI technologies.

AI's dual nature lies at the heart of its transformative potential:

- It can amplify human ingenuity, enabling us to solve problems that once seemed insurmountable—from improving healthcare to combating climate change.
- Without intentional oversight, it can also magnify biases, erode privacy, and create unforeseen risks.

An understanding of these dualities will equip you to make informed decisions about how to integrate AI into your life and work. Whether you're a developer, business leader, policymaker, or everyday user, the ethical use of AI depends on your commitment to thoughtful engagement.

In the future, one of AI's most profound impacts will be on the workforce. Automation and AI will reshape job roles, industries, and economic structures, displacing some roles while also creating new ones. This transformation is not just a technological shift, but a societal one, requiring proactive measures to ensure inclusivity, equity, and preparedness.

The challenges posed by this transition are immense, but so are the opportunities. AI has the potential to democratize access to knowledge, empower underrepresented groups, and drive economic growth if we approach it with foresight and intentionality. Chapter 7 will delve deeper into these economic impacts, exploring how we can prepare a diverse workforce to thrive in an AI-driven future.

The message of this chapter is simple, yet profound: *Stay informed, stay vigilant, and always strive to use AI in ways that align with ethical principles and human values.*

- **As an Individual:** Take time to understand the tools you use, question their outputs, and advocate for transparency and accountability.

- **As a Leader:** Equip your teams with the knowledge and frameworks to use AI responsibly, ensuring that decisions are aligned with broader ethical considerations.

- **As a Global Citizen:** Recognize the collective responsibility we share in shaping AI's role in society, from influencing policy to fostering inclusivity and sustainability.

By approaching AI with care and intention, you can harness its full potential to drive positive change, not just for yourself but also for the communities and systems you are part of.

AI is not just about technology; it's about people. It's about how we, as a society, choose to leverage tools that amplify our capabilities. As the orchestrators of this future, we must balance ambition with responsibility, curiosity with caution, and progress with ethics. By doing so, we can create a future where AI serves humanity, rather than the other way around.

Let this be the guiding principle as you continue your exploration in the next chapter, which examines the economic disruptions and opportunities AI may bring, and discusses ways to ensure that these changes benefit everyone.

7

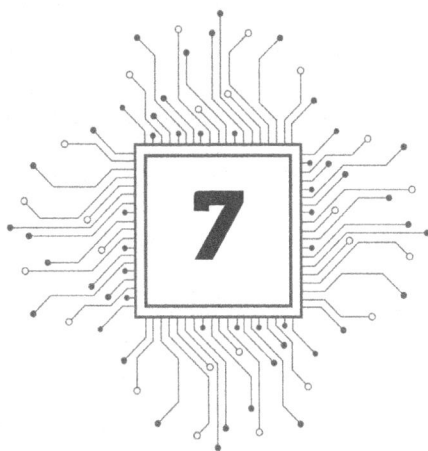

A Changing Tide: AI's Impact on Society

I began this book by sharing a story about my quest for information, which led me to switch rooms to access dial-up Internet as a teenager. By sharing that story, you could quickly identify the era I grew up in and when technology was introduced into my life.

Some may consider me a digital native—a term used to describe individuals exposed to digital technology such as the Internet and social media at a young age, making them native users of these technologies. However, I do not consider myself a digital native. I did not get a cell phone until I turned 18, and as we know from the story shared at the beginning of this book, my quest for Internet access was not very successful.

I feel as if I was born at the perfect time. Most of my childhood was lived without technology. It was a world defined by tactile experiences, human connection, and a slower, more reflective pace of life. When I stepped into the world for college, I was exposed to technology and its boundless potential. My world was split between two vastly different eras: one without technology as a child and one with technology as an adult. This dual perspective gave me an appreciation for both worlds and a deeper understanding of the way technology shapes, and reshapes, our lives.

Looking back, I realize how formative it was to experience a pre-digital childhood. Without screens to absorb my attention, I spent hours playing outside, creating imaginary worlds, and finding joy in simple moments. The quiet solitude of a book, the focus required to master piano pieces, and the hands-on curiosity of farm life shaped my sense of creativity and resilience. These experiences taught me patience, a skill that feels increasingly endangered in our hyper-connected world. Before the age of instant gratification, we learned to wait—to wait for dial-up to connect, for a library book to arrive, or for a letter to come in the mail. It's a form of waiting that also teaches reflection, anticipation, and presence.

When I entered the digital world, it felt like stepping into an endless sea of possibility. Suddenly, information wasn't something you had to hunt for; it was everywhere, waiting to be accessed with a click. Communication was instantaneous, and the boundaries of connection stretched across continents. But with this new accessibility came challenges: a constant barrage of notifications, a sense of pressure to always be "on," and the realization that my attention, once a private commodity, had become a sought-after currency for corporations.

This duality—living in both the pre-digital and digital worlds—offers a unique vantage point. I can still recall the sensory richness of a tech-free existence, yet I embrace the efficiencies and innovations that technology brings. For instance, I'm thankful for the way that technology enables global collaboration, helps automate mundane tasks, and unlocks access to education for millions. But I also see the downsides: the erosion of deep work, the rise of superficial connections, and the mental exhaustion that comes from always being plugged in.

Reflecting on this transitional period in my life, I can't help but wonder about today's youth. Born into a world of smartphones, streaming services, and AI, they've never known a life without the Internet. What will it mean for them to grow up in a world where answers are immediate, creativity is often augmented by algorithms, and connection comes with a double-edged sword of community and comparison? Will they develop the same patience, problem-solving skills, and creative depth that were once fostered by slower, analog experiences? Or will their strengths lie in entirely new areas, such as adaptability, digital fluency, and the ability to synthesize vast amounts of information?

My own journey from an analog childhood to a digital adulthood reminds me of a critical truth: Technology is neither inherently good nor bad; it is just a tool. Its impact on our lives depends entirely on how we wield it. The shift from pre-digital life to a digital world has brought incredible opportunities, but also created new challenges that demand thoughtful navigation. As we step further into the AI era, it's up to us to balance the promise of innovation with the preservation of what makes us uniquely human.

Digital Basics

The first job I ever had was at age 16, working as an "admin" at a funeral home. Growing up in the Midwest, in a town of fewer than 5,000 people, there weren't many job options for teenagers. I was fortunate that my parents knew the owner of a funeral home and could refer me for the job. My duties included keeping the funeral home "occupied" when no one was there, creating program flyers for ceremonies, processing death records, and once, driving the hearse. The last was a task I quickly realized I never wanted to repeat, especially as a 16-year-old who had just gotten my driver's license.

In hindsight, what stands out most from that job is how I first learned to process pictures and images. Despite the town's small size, there was steep competition among funeral homes, with more than three in the area. The funeral home I worked for was one of the newer ones, with a younger owner who was, I liked to think, the most tech-savvy of them all. One key service we offered was creating memorial videos. Families would bring in pictures of their deceased loved ones, which I would scan, order chronologically based on my own image detection skills, and compile into a slideshow with selected music.

This seemingly simple exercise taught me several things. First, it highlighted how quickly life passes and can be summarized into small moments captured in photos, which a high school student then scans and edits into a highlight reel. It made me realize that the moments we cherish most are usually with family and aren't particularly fancy but deeply meaningful. Each time I created a video, I saw that every life was incredibly beautiful yet fleeting, reminding me to savor every aspect of my own life.

From a technology perspective, I learned a crucial lesson about resizing images. When fitting a picture into a frame for a video, you must resize it from the corners to adjust both the height and width simultaneously. If you only pull from the top, bottom, or sides, the image will become distorted. Thankfully, before I could embarrass myself by releasing a video with lopsided images, the funeral home owner reviewed my work and taught me this essential technique.

Looking back, though, this process, while it felt innovative at the time, was quite rudimentary. I was working on a Windows 95 system using typical office tools such as PowerPoint, Word, a printer, and a scanner to copy the photos. The tools were limited, the process manual, and the margin for error high. And yet, it was a step forward—a glimpse of how technology could enhance even the most traditional industries.

Fast forward 25 years, and my work processes have changed beyond recognition. Today, when I create a movie, all my photos are already digital. There's no need for scanning; they're stored in the cloud, automatically backed up from my phone. My computer can access the cloud and instantly retrieve all the photos I need, neatly organized by date, location, or even the faces of people in the images. The tools for creating movies have evolved, too. Now, I use AI-assisted software like Descript, which allows me to add voiceovers, synchronize music, and make precise edits using natural language commands.

What once required hours of scanning, cropping, and manually syncing images to music now takes mere minutes. With AI, I can experiment with styles, automate transitions, and even generate captions, all without the technical expertise that used to be a prerequisite for video editing. This democratization of technology means that anyone, regardless of their background, can create something meaningful with the right tools.

I share this example to highlight a broader truth: No matter how long we've been working, whether it's our first job out of high school or our first corporate position, whether it's been 10 years or 50 years, the way we work has changed dramatically. And it's not just the tools that are different: The relationship we have with work has evolved alongside them.

When I reflect on my first job, I realize that technology then was a tool I needed to learn and adapt to, something external that enhanced my abilities but didn't define them. Today, technology, especially AI, feels more integrated into the process itself, a seamless collaborator rather than just a tool. This shift raises fascinating questions: How much of our work do we want technology to handle? At what point does it stop being an assistant and start becoming a driver of our creative processes? And how do we maintain a balance between efficiency and the deeper, human-centered meaning of the work we do?

As the tools we use grow more intelligent, they also challenge us to evolve, not just in how we work, but also in how we think about work. My journey from PowerPoint slides on a Windows 95 system to AI-assisted video editing mirrors a larger societal transition: from manual processes to automation, from rigid systems to adaptive ones, and from isolated tasks to interconnected workflows. The key is not to view these changes as a threat, but rather to embrace them as an opportunity to rethink what's possible, for ourselves and for the work we leave behind.

Exercise: Reflecting on the Evolution of Work

The way we work has evolved dramatically over time, influenced by advances in technology, shifts in societal expectations, and the growing demand for efficiency and creativity. At this point, I encourage you to take a moment to reflect on how your own relationship with work has changed, whether through tools, processes, or even the roles you've taken on.

For this exercise, you can use a notepad, iPad, or even a blank piece of paper—whatever medium feels most comfortable. The goal is to reflect thoughtfully on whether you identify as a digital native, an analog enthusiast, or somewhere in between.

1. First Job

- **Think back to your first job.** What was it, and how did you approach the work? Did technology play any role in your tasks, or was it more manual? For example, did you use paper files, a basic computer system, or tools specific to that job?

- **What skills did you learn?** Reflect on the habits, problem-solving approaches, or techniques you developed. How did these shape the way you approached work in your later roles?

- **How did this work make you feel?** Consider the emotional connection you had to this role. Were you eager to learn, or did the work feel repetitive?

2. First Corporate Job

- **How did your first corporate job differ from your first job?** Think about the scale, the structure, and the expectations. Was technology more integrated, or did you still find yourself relying on manual processes?

- **What tools or systems did you use?** For instance, did you work with early databases, proprietary software, or rudimentary tools like spreadsheets? Were there technologies that felt cutting-edge at the time?

- **What challenges did you face?** Reflect on any difficulties you encountered in adapting to corporate workflows or new technology. Did you feel adequately prepared, or did you have to learn on the job?

3. Current Work

- **Compare the processes of your current work to your earlier roles.** How have tools, workflows, or technologies evolved? Are there tasks you can now accomplish in minutes that used to take hours?

- **What role does technology play today?** Think about the AI-driven tools, cloud-based platforms, or advanced systems you may use. How do these technologies enhance or complicate your work?

- **What has stayed the same?** While much has likely changed, some aspects of work, such as collaboration, creativity, and discipline, may remain constant. Reflect on these enduring elements and their importance in your current role.

Deeper Reflection

Once you've considered these questions, take a moment to think about the following aspects of your work life:

- **Your adaptability.** How have you grown as a worker through these transitions? Which skills have you gained, and how have your perspectives on work evolved?

- **The tools you depend on.** Which technologies do you rely on most, and how would your work change if they were suddenly unavailable?

- **Your relationship with technology.** Do you see technology as a collaborator, a tool, or a challenge to navigate? How has this relationship influenced your approach to work?

The purpose of this exercise is not only to recognize how far you've come, but also to connect your personal journey with the broader evolution of work in society. By reflecting on these transitions, you can gain insights into how technology has shaped your career, and how you can continue to adapt and thrive in an ever-changing landscape.

A Constant of Change

No matter if you started your job five years ago, 10 years ago, 25 years ago, or 50 years ago, the way we work has drastically changed. As Heraclitus famously said, "The only constant in life is change." Yet, the changes we're experiencing today feel different—more rapid, more disruptive, and, for many people, more unsettling. Why do these changes elicit such a visceral reaction? I believe the discomfort stems from two core areas: the accelerating pace of change and the challenge that AI poses to what we as humans have long regarded as our most defining advantage, our intelligence.

As described in earlier chapters, humans have always created tools to evolve. These tools don't just solve problems; they redefine what's possible. Each invention also builds on the last, compounding the pace of innovation. Consider the last four Industrial Revolutions as a case in point.

The first Industrial Revolution began in the 1780s, ushering in a world powered by machinery, water, and steam. This revolution spanned decades, allowing society time to adapt to the changes it brought. The second Industrial Revolution, which introduced mass production, assembly lines, and electricity in the 1900s, transformed industries and created efficiencies that reshaped daily life. Then came the third Industrial Revolution, centered on computers and automation. Many of us grew up in this era, watching as tasks once performed manually became digitized and streamlined. Finally, the fourth Industrial Revolution, beginning in the early 2000s, brought the rise of the Internet, interconnected systems, and cyber-physical environments.

What is most striking about these revolutions is the decreasing time between them. Moving from the first to the second Industrial Revolution took about 120 years. The leap to the third Industrial Revolution required only 70 years, and advancing to the fourth took just 30 years. Now, as we stand on the precipice of a fifth Industrial Revolution, defined by AI, biotechnology, and quantum computing, the pace of change has accelerated so much that revolutions seem to overlap.

For someone born in the 1780s, the notion of witnessing even a single Industrial Revolution was unlikely, not just due to the shorter life spans but because these transformations spanned centuries. Today, it's not uncommon for individuals to live through multiple Industrial Revolutions within their lifetime. For younger generations, this accelerating rate of change means the skills and tools they learn today could be obsolete before their careers reach maturity.

The Psychological Impact of Rapid Change

Although humans may not like change, our adaptability is one of the reasons we've thrived as a species. When faced with new environments, challenges, and opportunities, we innovate, collaborate, and persevere. However, the nature of this current shift, which is driven by the rise of AI, feels uniquely challenging. Why? Because it targets the very thing we've long used to define ourselves: our intellect.

Human dominance has never been rooted in physical strength or speed. We've succeeded because of our larger, more developed neocortex, which grants us the ability to engage in higher cognitive functions like abstract thinking, problem solving, and creativity. This intelligence enabled humans to create tools, write poetry, build civilizations, and pursue scientific discovery. Until the advent of AI, our intelligence had never been questioned, by ourselves or by any other species. Now, as machines begin to outperform humans in tasks that require reasoning, analysis, and creativity, it's natural to question our own value.

This line of questioning often intersects with our sense of work and purpose. While you can scroll through LinkedIn on any given day and find people lamenting their jobs, work–life balance, or the grind of corporate life, most of us hold our work dearly. For the vast majority, work serves as a means to an end, providing financial stability and supporting our families. But for many, work also represents something deeper: a sense of identity, purpose, and achievement. It's not just about what we do; it's about who we are.

Why AI Feels So Threatening

This is why the rise of AI feels so profoundly unsettling. It's not just about automation replacing routine tasks; it's about the fear of losing our place in the world. If machines can write novels, diagnose illnesses, compose music, or design buildings, what does that mean for the human spirit? For centuries, humans have tied our worth to our ability to think, create, and innovate. AI challenges that notion—not by threatening to destroy us, as dystopian narratives suggest, but rather by forcing us to reconsider what makes us unique.

However, framing AI as a threat limits both our imagination and our progress. This mindset risks leaving people behind, stuck in outdated paradigms and unable to harness the opportunities AI presents. AI is not here to replace us; it's here to augment us. It's not an adversary but a collaborator—one that's ready to help us create, explore, and evolve in ways we've never imagined.

The key is reframing the narrative. Instead of seeing AI as a rival, we should view it as an extension of our own capabilities—as a tool that enhances human creativity and productivity rather than diminishing it. Throughout history, every major technological advancement has been met with skepticism and fear. When electricity was first introduced, people worried about its dangers; when computers became mainstream, fears of job loss arose. Yet each of these innovations ultimately improved our lives and expanded what we could achieve. AI, though more complex and disruptive, is no different.

Moving Forward Together

As we navigate this transition, it's essential to recognize both the challenges and the opportunities AI brings. Yes, the speed of change is overwhelming, and yes, AI will reshape industries and displace certain jobs. But it will also create new possibilities, unlock new industries, and redefine the very nature of work.

The question we must ask ourselves is not "Will AI replace us?" but rather "How can we use AI to elevate what we do best?" By embracing AI as a partner, we can preserve what makes us human—our empathy, intuition, and creativity—while leveraging its power to solve problems, enhance efficiency, and unlock new horizons.

Change may be constant, but so is our capacity to adapt. By leaning into this new era with curiosity and courage, we can ensure that AI serves as a catalyst for a brighter, more innovative future.

How AI Is "Actually" Changing Work

While the term **artificial general intelligence (AGI)** is loosely defined, a common interpretation is that it refers to a system capable of surpassing human abilities across a broad range of cognitive tasks, including reasoning, problem solving, and decision making. However, as we've discussed in previous chapters, today's AI is not AGI but **narrow AI**, which is designed to excel at specific tasks. Understanding this distinction is crucial when evaluating how AI is transforming work: Wholesale job replacement is not occurring, but rather a profound shift in how we complete individual tasks.

The World Economic Forum's *Future of Jobs Report* (2023) highlighted this dynamic. It revealed that in 2022, machines performed 34% of tasks compared to 66% by humans. By 2027, that balance is projected to shift to 43% machine tasks and 57% human tasks. Naturally, this data raises concerns: Does a 10% increase in machine-driven task share equate to a 10% reduction in jobs? The answer is far more nuanced. These percentages refer to *tasks*, not entire roles, and the implications are far more complex than a simple one-to-one substitution.

The Nature of Tasks in Jobs

An analysis conducted by the Human Machine Collaboration Institute offers valuable insights. Across 80 distinct job descriptions, we identified a total of 1,365 discrete tasks. However, these job descriptions rarely quantified the time or significance of each task within the broader scope of the role. For example:

- A task like "communicating updates to a team" may take just a few minutes but recur multiple times a day.
- By contrast, a task like "developing a strategic plan" might consume several hours or even weeks, but occur less frequently.

This distinction is critical when interpreting the impacts of AI. Automation may streamline smaller, repetitive tasks, freeing up time for humans to focus on strategic, creative, or interpersonal work. At the same time, AI may augment longer, complex tasks, helping with research, analysis, or drafting, rather than fully automating them.

Tasks Versus Jobs: The Key Distinction

When people hear statistics about AI's growing role in task completion, one question often arises: *Will this lead to job loss?* The answer requires an understanding of a workplace reality: Jobs are not monolithic. Most roles are composed of a mix of tasks, and automation rarely replaces every component. Instead, AI changes the nature of how work is performed, often creating opportunities for workers to specialize, innovate, or engage in higher-value activities.

Historical trends illustrate this point. In the early 1800s, nearly 80% of the U.S. workforce was employed in farming. By the early 1900s, that figure had dropped to 40%, and today it's in the single digits. Yet this shift did not result in mass unemployment. Instead, it spurred the development of entirely new industries—manufacturing, services, and technology—that provided millions of jobs in areas unimaginable to earlier generations.

Similarly, projections for AI's impact on employment reveal both challenges and opportunities. It's estimated that AI could replace 92 million jobs globally by 2030. On the flip side, it has the potential to create 170 million new roles. These roles will likely span emerging fields like AI ethics, data annotation, human–machine collaboration, and AI operations.

The Imperative for Upskilling and Reskilling

The key to navigating this transition lies in **upskilling** and **reskilling**. While humans have always adapted to technological shifts, the current rate of change is faster than ever before. In the past, societies had decades, even centuries, to transition from one dominant form of work to another. Today, workers must adapt within years, often while still performing their existing roles.

To illustrate this need, consider the agricultural revolution that reduced the number of farming jobs. While that shift took place over more than a century, today's technological disruptions, such as the shift from manual to digital workflows and the rise of AI, can transform entire industries in less than a decade. This accelerated timeline necessitates proactive efforts from governments, businesses, and educational institutions to equip workers with the skills they need for a future shaped by AI.

Upskilling involves enhancing existing skills, such as learning how to use AI tools in the individual's current role. For example:

- A marketer might adopt AI-driven platforms like ChatGPT or HubSpot AI to personalize campaigns at scale.
- A project manager might use AI tools for predictive analytics, optimizing workflows, or automating routine updates.

Reskilling, by comparison, focuses on training workers for entirely new roles. Consider someone in a manual data entry role transitioning to become a data analyst or someone in a manufacturing role learning to operate and maintain AI-powered robotics.

Preparing for the Future of Work

The shift to AI-driven task completion doesn't mean that all jobs are safe. Some roles will inevitably become obsolete, particularly those reliant on repetitive, rules-based tasks. However, this isn't a new phenomenon; it's a continuation of a pattern that has defined human progress for centuries. The difference today is the speed at which this transformation is unfolding, and the scale of the global economy it's impacting.

To navigate this change successfully, we need to focus on three key areas:

- **Education and Training:** Schools, universities, and corporate training programs must prioritize AI literacy and teach workers how to collaborate effectively with machines.

- **Policy and Infrastructure:** Governments must invest in policies that support lifelong learning, provide safety nets for displaced workers, and encourage the development of new industries.

- **Mindset and Resilience:** As individuals, we must cultivate a growth mindset, embracing change as an opportunity rather than a threat. The ability to learn, adapt, and innovate will be the most valuable skill in the AI era.

Embracing Human–AI Collaboration

Ultimately, AI's impact on work is not about machines replacing humans but about redefining roles in ways that can unlock human potential. By automating repetitive tasks and augmenting complex ones, AI frees us to focus on what we do best—problem solving, creativity, empathy, and innovation.

The transition may be challenging, but it's also an opportunity to rethink the nature of work itself. What if the future of work isn't about doing more, but rather about doing better? What if AI allows us to focus on work that brings purpose and fulfillment while machines handle the mundane? These are the possibilities we must explore as we navigate the era of AI-powered transformation.

Making the Transition

Most importantly, what does this mean for you? How do you ensure that you're on the side of the job being created rather than the one being replaced?

By reading this book, you are already ahead of the curve, not just because it's my book, but because of your *curiosity*. You're interested in how AI can be integrated into your workflow and open to exploring new ways of thinking and working. This openness is perhaps the most fundamental and often overlooked step. Curiosity is not just a personal quality; it's a strategic advantage in times of rapid change. And in this new age of AI, it is curiosity, combined with adaptability, that will set you apart.

While many of the new jobs created by AI have yet to be defined, it's tempting to believe that the only way forward is to jump headfirst into AI-specific roles such as machine learning engineer, data scientist, or AI specialist. While these are exciting and high-demand fields, they're not the only paths to success in this evolving landscape. In fact, I believe there's a better approach for most people—*incorporating AI into your current workstreams, passions, and interests.*

Finding Your Place in the AI-Driven World

History shows us that every major technological shift creates opportunities far beyond its core field. When social media platforms like Instagram, Facebook, and Twitter (now X) first emerged, the focus was on building the technology itself. Everyone wanted to create the next big platform, and while a few succeeded, many more failed. What wasn't immediately obvious was the ecosystem of jobs that would grow around these platforms: content creators, social media managers, influencers, digital marketers, and even meme strategists. These roles weren't anticipated at the outset, but they became integral to the platforms' success.

AI is no different. While it's essential to have experts designing and refining AI systems, the real revolution lies in *how we use those systems.* AI is a tool, a powerful one, but its value will ultimately be determined by the people who find innovative ways to apply it. For example:

- Healthcare professionals are leveraging AI to improve patient outcomes by analyzing data for early diagnoses and personalized treatment plans.
- Teachers are using AI to create tailored lesson plans and engage students with interactive, adaptive learning tools.
- Entrepreneurs are harnessing AI to streamline business processes, automate customer service, and uncover new market opportunities.

These are just a few examples of how AI can enhance existing fields. The possibilities are vast, and they extend far beyond the scope of AI development itself.

Embrace Your Unique Approach

To stay ahead of the curve, the key is not to follow the crowd but to carve your own path. It's easy to feel pressure to upskill in AI algorithms, coding, or data science because that's where the spotlight is.

But history has shown that the greatest opportunities often lie in the applications of the core technology, rather than in the technology itself. Instead of asking, "How can I become an AI expert?" ask, *How can I use AI to enhance what I already love to do?*

For example:

- If you're a creative professional, AI can help you brainstorm ideas, automate tedious editing tasks, or explore entirely new art forms.
- If you work in finance, AI can analyze data patterns to provide faster, more accurate insights for decision making.
- If you're in customer service, AI-powered chatbots and sentiment analysis tools can help you focus on resolving complex issues while automating routine queries.

The most exciting part is that these tools allow you to focus on what truly matters—your passion, creativity, and ability to solve problems. By integrating AI into your workflow, you're amplifying (not replacing) your skills.

The Power of Curiosity

One of the questions I most frequently hear is "How can I ensure I'm not automated?" The technical answers, such as upskilling, learning AI orchestration, and analyzing workflows, are certainly important. However, the most critical answer is this: *Curiosity is your key.* Trying new tools, experimenting with new processes, and staying open to change is your superpower.

We often overlook the value of experimentation because it feels inefficient or risky. But experimentation is where the real breakthroughs happen. Think about the creators of Airbnb, who reimagined the hospitality industry, or the founders of Canva, who democratized graphic design. They didn't start by asking, "How do I become a software engineer?" They started by asking, "What problem can I solve?" They then used the tools available to bring their vision to life.

AI is your tool. The question now is, *What will you build with it?*

A Playbook for the New Age

To thrive in the age of AI, focus on the guiding principles explained here and in Figure 7.1.

- **Stay Curious:** Regularly explore new AI tools and applications. Treat them as opportunities to enhance—not replace—your abilities.

- **Embrace Lifelong Learning:** Commit to continuous upskilling in your field, whether it's mastering AI-enabled tools or learning adjacent skills that complement your expertise.

- **Follow Your Passion:** Use AI to deepen your engagement with the work you love. Whether you're in the arts, business, science, or education, there's a way to incorporate AI that aligns with your interests.

- **Innovate Within Your Space:** Instead of pivoting to AI itself, think about how AI can transform your current industry or role. The best ideas often come from those who combine domain expertise with emerging technology.

- **Adopt a Growth Mindset:** View challenges as opportunities to grow. The most successful individuals in this era will be those who see change as a chance to reinvent themselves.

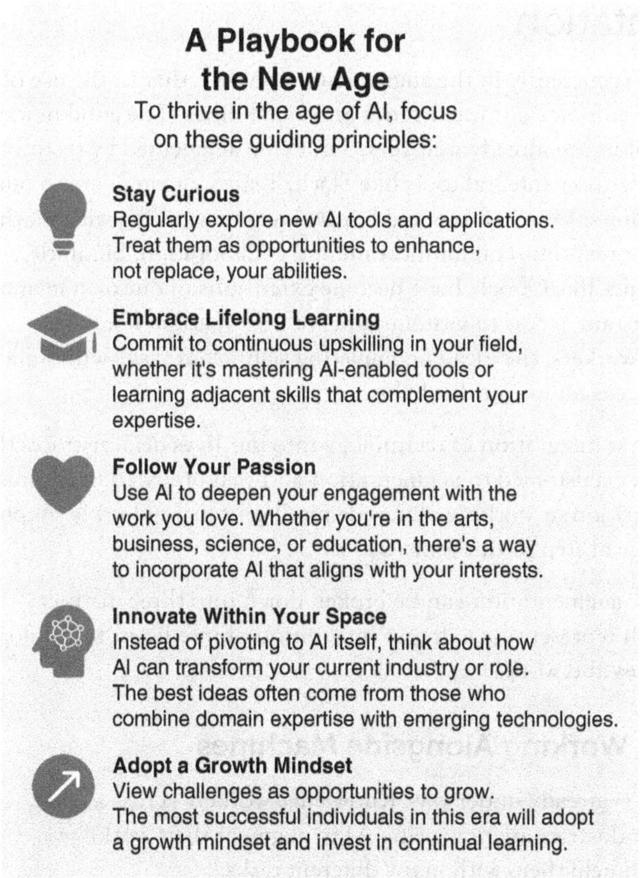

A Playbook for
the New Age
To thrive in the age of AI, focus
on these guiding principles:

Stay Curious
Regularly explore new AI tools and applications.
Treat them as opportunities to enhance,
not replace, your abilities.

Embrace Lifelong Learning
Commit to continuous upskilling in your field,
whether it's mastering AI-enabled tools or
learning adjacent skills that complement your
expertise.

Follow Your Passion
Use AI to deepen your engagement with the
work you love. Whether you're in the arts,
business, science, or education, there's a way
to incorporate AI that aligns with your interests.

Innovate Within Your Space
Instead of pivoting to AI itself, think about how
AI can transform your current industry or role.
The best ideas often come from those who
combine domain expertise with emerging technologies.

Adopt a Growth Mindset
View challenges as opportunities to grow.
The most successful individuals in this era will adopt
a growth mindset and invest in continual learning.

FIGURE 7.1 How to Thrive in the Age of AI

Moving Forward with Confidence

The AI revolution is not something to fear; it's something to embrace. Like every technological shift before it, this one will create new challenges, but it will also unlock unprecedented opportunities. By staying curious, taking risks, and pursuing what excites you, you can ensure that you're not merely part of the change but a driver of it.

You don't need to be an AI expert to thrive in this era. You just need to ask the right questions, seek out the right tools, and trust in your ability to adapt. Remember, *curiosity is your key, experimentation is your superpower, and your unique approach is your differentiator*. The future of work isn't about being replaced; it's about being empowered to do what you love better than ever before.

Augmentation

The AI era is currently in the **augmentation** phase—that is, the use of using AI to enhance our intelligence and capabilities. The good news is that most of us are already well versed in being augmented by technology. Consider how integral tools like Slack, Teams, or email are to our daily workflows. Many of us could hardly imagine working without these channels for real-time communication and collaboration. Similarly, search engines like Google have become extensions of our own memory, giving us instant access to vast amounts of information. For most knowledge workers, the idea of completing significant tasks without a digital device is almost unthinkable.

This seamless integration of technology into our lives demonstrates that we are both accustomed to augmentation and well prepared to embrace it. The transition to working alongside intelligent technology is simply the next logical step in this journey.

The path of augmentation can be broken down into three distinct phases, each representing a deeper integration of intelligent technology into our lives and work.

Phase 1: Working Alongside Machines

This phase is already under way. Knowledge workers across a wide variety of industries are now using AI to augment their workflows. AI tools can help them with many different tasks:

- Automating email responses with tools like Gmail's Smart Compose

- Generating ideas and drafting content with tools like ChatGPT
- Analyzing data patterns with platforms like Tableau or Power BI

For example, in creative industries, AI tools like Adobe Firefly are helping designers generate mockups and explore variations faster than ever. In healthcare, AI-powered systems are assisting doctors by analyzing medical imaging to identify potential anomalies that might be missed by the human eye.

This phase isn't about replacing human intelligence, but rather amplifying it. Machines handle the repetitive and mundane, while humans focus on tasks that require creativity, critical thinking, and empathy. This collaboration allows us to scale our abilities and achieve more than we ever could alone.

Phase 2: Transitioning Tasks to Intelligent Machines

In this next phase, we'll see a shift as more tasks are transitioned to intelligent machines, whether they're software agents for knowledge workers or robotics for manual labor jobs. This transition will enable us to focus on higher-order tasks while machines take over routine, time-consuming, or dangerous work.

Examples of this phase include:

- **Software Agents:** Imagine AI assistants scheduling meetings, summarizing documents, or even drafting policies tailored to specific company guidelines. Tools like Otter.ai can already transcribe meetings in real time, and future iterations could summarize action items or even draft follow-up emails.
- **Physical Robotics:** In industries like construction and manufacturing, robots are performing tasks like bricklaying, welding, and assembling components with precision and efficiency. Drones are being deployed for tasks like inspecting infrastructure or delivering goods to remote locations.

This phase will also see the emergence of **AI-powered agents** working autonomously on behalf of humans. These agents could handle entire workflows, from generating reports to managing customer interactions. Importantly, this shift doesn't mean the elimination of jobs, but instead the evolution of roles. Workers will increasingly become managers of these intelligent systems, overseeing and guiding their outputs.

Phase 3: Learning from Machines

The final phase of augmentation will fundamentally change how we understand ourselves. In this stage, humans will begin learning from machines, leveraging their ability to process and analyze data to uncover insights that were previously inaccessible.

We're already seeing the early stages of this phase with advances in neuroscience and brain–computer interfaces. For instance:

- **Decoding Thought Patterns:** Studies have used AI algorithms to analyze brain activity and decode a song someone is thinking about from their fMRI (functional magnetic resonance imaging) data. Such breakthroughs could lead to new ways of understanding human thought and emotion.

- **Health Insights:** Wearable devices like Apple Watches and Fitbits provide basic health data, but this is just the beginning. Future technologies could offer insights into mental health, stress levels, or even early indicators of disease by analyzing subtle changes in our physiology.

Imagine a future where technology goes beyond just tracking your steps or heart rate to provide a comprehensive analysis of your well-being, highlighting how your diet, sleep patterns, and stress levels interact to influence your mental and physical health. These insights could revolutionize preventive medicine, personal development, and even our understanding of consciousness.

In this phase, the line between technology and humanity will become blurred as machines help us uncover the mysteries of our own existence. But we won't be surrendering our humanity to machines; instead, we'll be using their capabilities to deepen our understanding of what it means to be human.

A Glimpse into the Future

These three phases—working alongside machines, transitioning tasks to intelligent systems, and learning from machines—represent a journey of deepening collaboration between humans and AI. At each step, our role evolves, but one thing remains constant: our ability to adapt and thrive.

In Chapter 8, we'll dive into what this means in terms of the future of work and the role of the AI Orchestrator. As you'll see, becoming an Orchestrator is not just about managing technology, but also about mastering the art of collaboration—between humans, machines, and the opportunities they create together.

Conclusion

In this chapter, we explored the profound ways in which AI is reshaping not just our work, but also the fabric of society. From the early days of rudimentary digital tools to the sophisticated AI-driven systems of today, one constant remains: the power of human adaptation and evolution. Work processes have already been dramatically transformed, and the rapid pace of technological advancement ensures that this trend will continue to accelerate, challenging and empowering us in equal measure.

AI's impact on our jobs is not about replacement but augmentation, enhancing our capabilities, amplifying our potential, and creating new pathways for innovation. By staying curious, embracing new tools, and committing to lifelong learning, we can successfully navigate the transition to this AI-augmented world.

The phases of augmentation illustrate a compelling trajectory:

• *Working alongside machines*, as AI collaborates with us to streamline workflows and improve outcomes.

• *Transitioning tasks to intelligent systems*, freeing us from routine tasks to focus on creativity, strategy, and empathy.

• *Learning from machines*, unlocking deeper insights into our own humanity and creating opportunities for personal and collective growth.

As we move forward, the key to thriving lies in our ability to *integrate these technologies into our work and lives thoughtfully*. This is not about merely keeping pace with change, but also entails leading the charge, using AI as a tool to shape the future of work in ways that reflect our values, passions, and aspirations.

This journey of augmentation presents a profound opportunity. It invites us to grow beyond old paradigms, to approach work with renewed creativity, and to achieve levels of progress once considered unimaginable. The challenges that lie ahead are significant, but the potential for transformation is even greater.

In the next chapter, we'll delve deeper into what it means to actively shape the future. We'll explore the continuous evolution of work and how each of us can become an Orchestrator, a leader in this new era of AI and human collaboration. Together, we'll uncover how to embrace this transformative moment not just as participants, but as pioneers.

8

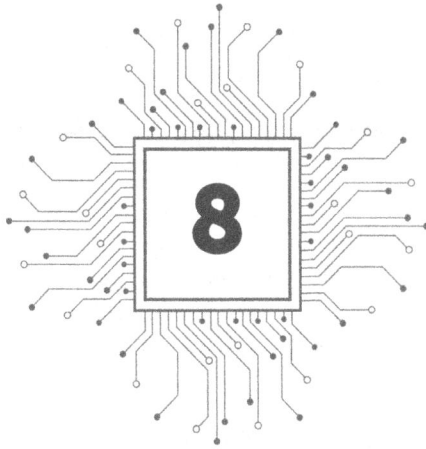

Shaping the Future as an Orchestrator

In Chapter 7, we discussed how AI is reshaping the workforce. While AI currently excels at supporting tasks, it hasn't yet reached the point where it can fully take over entire jobs. However, with the rapid pace of technological advancement, that may soon change. So, what does this mean for us as humans? Will we be displaced from work entirely? Or can we look to history to uncover patterns that might guide us forward?

Lessons from History: Jevons Paradox and the Luddites

To understand the potential outcomes of widespread AI adoption, we can draw on economic history. One relevant concept is **Jevons paradox**, which occurs when technological progress increases the efficiency of resource use, but the resulting decrease in cost triggers greater demand, ultimately leading to higher overall consumption.

A classic example is the invention of the steam engine in the 19th century. The steam engine significantly improved the efficiency of coal use. However, instead of reducing coal consumption, it spurred greater demand for coal-powered applications. Similarly, the rise of personal computers didn't reduce our reliance on computing power, but rather exponentially increased it, fueling the development of new industries, products, and services.

In the context of AI, Jevons paradox suggests that as AI systems become more efficient, they won't necessarily reduce the need for human input or jobs. Instead, they'll create *new demand* for AI-enhanced goods and services, opening up opportunities for roles we haven't yet imagined. This paradox points to a future of abundance where productivity gains drive down costs and increase access, but it also challenges us to adapt rapidly to new forms of work.

The Historical Parallel: The Luddites

Another historical example is the **Luddite movement** of the early 19th century. These English textile workers, who were skilled in traditional crafts, destroyed mechanized looms and other machinery that threatened their livelihoods. The Luddites feared that machines would render their skills obsolete, lower wages, and lead to inferior goods. They weren't entirely wrong: Mechanization did disrupt their industry. However, the broader outcome was transformative: The Industrial Revolution laid the foundation for modern manufacturing, which created new jobs, industries, and economic opportunities.

Fast forward to today, and we see echoes of the Luddite fears in discussions around AI. Concerns about job displacement, wage reduction, and skill redundancy are widespread. But history offers hope. While the Luddites may have lost their battle, the technological progress they

opposed eventually benefited society at large. It gave rise to higher productivity, cheaper goods, and entirely new sectors of employment.

The question is, *Will history repeat itself with AI?*

The AI Era: Will History Repeat Itself?

AI differs from past technological revolutions in one key way: It targets
cognitive tasks rather than physical ones. This shift creates a deeper
existential concern, as AI begins to challenge what many believe to be
the essence of human work—our ability to think, reason, and create.
While the Luddites feared losing jobs based on physical labor, today's
workers worry about losing roles that require intellect, judgment, and
emotional intelligence.

But history suggests a pattern that may apply here: *Disruption is painful,
but it also drives innovation.* The rise of AI is unlikely to be any different.
We may see a period of upheaval as industries restructure, but this will
pave the way for new opportunities:

- **Expanding the Scope of Human Creativity:** AI can handle routine or
  repetitive cognitive tasks, freeing humans to focus on higher-order
  thinking and creative endeavors.
- **Unlocking New Industries:** Just as the Internet gave rise to roles like
  web developers and social media managers, AI will create jobs in
  fields like AI ethics, human–AI interaction, and AI orchestration.
- **Reducing Barriers to Entry:** AI can democratize access to tools and
  resources, enabling individuals without formal training to achieve
  professional-quality results in fields like design, analysis, and content
  creation.

The challenge lies in navigating this transition thoughtfully,
ensuring that we adapt without leaving significant portions of the
workforce behind.

The Role of the Orchestrator

As we shape the future, one of the most critical roles will be that of the
AI Orchestrator. The individuals filling this role will aim to manage
the interaction between humans and machines to maximize efficiency,
creativity, and impact. As such, this role requires a deep understanding
of both human capabilities and AI systems, bridging the gap between
technology and its practical application.

An Orchestrator is not merely a technical expert but a visionary who can do the following:

- **Anticipate Shifts in Workflows:** Understand which tasks are best handled by humans, machines, or a combination of both.
- **Guide Ethical AI Use:** Ensure that AI systems are deployed responsibly, with considerations for fairness, transparency, and inclusivity.
- **Foster Collaboration:** Encourage teams to embrace AI as a tool for augmentation rather than a replacement.

In essence, the Orchestrator will be a leader in this new era of work—someone who not only adapts to change, but also helps others navigate and thrive during the transition.

Preparing for What's Next

While the concerns surrounding AI are valid, they are not insurmountable. The lessons of Jevons paradox and the Luddites remind us that technological disruption may be viewed as both a challenge and an opportunity. As AI continues to evolve, it will create new demands, new industries, and new ways of working. The key to shaping this future lies in our willingness to adapt, learn, and innovate in this context.

Will we encounter the same fate as the Luddites? Perhaps the better question is, *How can we ensure a better outcome?* By embracing the role of Orchestrator, we can guide this transition, balancing the power of AI with the irreplaceable value of human ingenuity and empathy. Working together, we can ensure that history doesn't just repeat itself, but evolves in positive ways.

An Abundant Future

The possibilities AI brings to create an abundant and prosperous future are vast. By enhancing productivity, accelerating scientific discovery, and personalizing education, AI offers a path to improve the quality of life for people around the world. Let's explore how this vision of abundance might unfold.

Increased Productivity and Economic Growth

As discussed in connection with the Jevons paradox, AI has the potential to significantly boost productivity while simultaneously reducing the cost of goods and services. By automating routine tasks and augmenting human capabilities, AI can transform industries and unlock new levels of efficiency. This increased productivity could ripple across the global economy, fueling growth and fostering innovation on a worldwide basis.

For example:

- **Agriculture:** AI-powered systems could optimize crop yields by analyzing weather patterns, soil quality, and plant health. Drones equipped with AI could monitor and tend to crops more efficiently, helping reduce food scarcity and improve nutrition worldwide.
- **Manufacturing:** AI-driven robotics and predictive maintenance tools could reduce downtime and improve production rates, making goods more affordable and accessible.
- **Logistics and Supply Chains:** Algorithms that predict demand and optimize routes could minimize waste and ensure goods are delivered faster and cheaper.

Perhaps most excitingly, AI could drive breakthroughs in areas traditionally constrained by human limitations, such as medical research, clean energy, and materials science. These advances could address some of humanity's most pressing challenges, from curing diseases to combating climate change.

Scientific and Medical Advances

AI's potential to revolutionize science and medicine is already evident. One of the most groundbreaking examples is Google's AlphaFold, which solved the decades-old problem of protein structure prediction. This achievement has accelerated drug discovery and deepened our understanding of biological processes.

Looking ahead, AI could lead to the following gains in this area:

- **Faster Drug Development:** AI models can analyze vast datasets to identify promising compounds, predict their efficacy, and even simulate clinical trials, dramatically shortening the time it takes to bring new treatments to market.
- **Precision Medicine:** By analyzing genetic data and patient histories, AI can help create personalized treatment plans tailored to an individual's unique needs.
- **Clean Energy Breakthroughs:** AI-powered simulations can explore the effectiveness and efficiency of new materials for batteries, solar cells, and other energy technologies, accelerating the transition to renewable energy sources.

These advancements could significantly improve human health, extend lifespans, and address global challenges that have eluded solutions for centuries.

Personalized Education and Skills Development

As someone passionate about education, I'm particularly excited about AI's potential to transform how we learn. The advent of the Internet has already democratized access to knowledge through platforms like Coursera, Udemy, edX, and YouTube. However, these systems are often one-size-fits-all solutions, leaving many learners struggling to find the right class, at the right time, for the right job. AI has the potential to bridge this gap by offering highly personalized learning experiences.

AI tutoring systems, such as Khanmigo from Khan Academy, are already paving the way for tailored educational experiences. These systems adapt to each learner's unique needs, providing guidance, feedback, and encouragement. Unlike traditional methods, AI tutors can:

- Identify knowledge gaps and recommend targeted exercises.
- Adjust pacing to match the learner's comfort level.
- Provide explanations in multiple ways to suit different learning styles.

On a personal level, I've experienced the transformative power of AI in education. As I learn French, tools like ChatGPT have been invaluable. Speaking a new language aloud can be daunting: You worry about mispronunciations or sounding foolish. But interacting with an AI model feels safe. It is patient, nonjudgmental, and always ready to provide constructive feedback. This kind of supportive environment fosters confidence and accelerates progress.

Unlocking Human Potential

AI's ability to create personalized learning pathways doesn't just make education more effective; it makes it more enjoyable. Imagine a world where learning is fun, where barriers like fear of failure are replaced with encouragement and progress feels natural. Whether it's helping a student overcome math anxiety or enabling a professional to upskill for a new role, AI can empower individuals to reach their full potential.

Moreover, AI can expand access to quality education for underserved communities. Imagine students in remote areas receiving one-on-one instruction through AI tutors or professionals in developing countries, thereby gaining skills that make them competitive in the global market.

By breaking down barriers to education, AI has the potential to level the playing field and reduce inequality.

Automation of Dangerous or Undesirable Jobs

One of the most promising applications of AI and robotics lies in automating dangerous or undesirable jobs. While we've only just begun to see this potential take root, the implications are profound. Imagine a future where no one has to perform tasks that are physically hazardous, emotionally draining, or mind-numbingly repetitive. AI and robotics can serve as powerful tools to not only improve efficiency but also enhance human well-being by freeing people from jobs they dislike or that put them at risk.

Eliminating Repetitive and Mindless Tasks

In my conversations with professionals across industries, I often hear a recurring theme: Despite landing the job titles they've long desired at their dream companies, many individuals find themselves performing tedious, repetitive tasks. These onerous duties can range from manually copying and pasting data between systems to repetitive form-filling or administrative work. These tasks, while necessary, add little value to human potential.

AI offers an easy win here. By automating such processes, we can not only improve productivity but also allow individuals to focus on more meaningful, creative, and fulfilling work. This shift promises to be especially impactful in knowledge-based roles where the drudgery of mundane tasks often stifles innovation and job satisfaction.

Addressing Dangerous Jobs

AI and robotics also hold immense promise in automating physically dangerous roles. Consider industries like mining, construction, and firefighting, where workers face significant risks daily. Robotic systems equipped with AI can take over tasks such as inspecting unstable structures, performing search-and-rescue operations in hazardous conditions, or handling toxic materials. This doesn't just reduce risk; it saves lives.

For example:

• **Mining:** Autonomous machinery can perform underground drilling and extraction without putting human lives in harm's way.

- **Disaster Response:** Drones powered by AI can assess damage, locate survivors, and deliver aid in disaster-stricken areas faster and more safely than humans.

- **Nuclear Cleanup:** Robots like those used in Fukushima, Japan, following the earthquake/tsunami-induced nuclear disaster there have been deployed to handle radioactive materials—a task no human could safely perform.

Automating these roles does more than simply improve safety. It opens the door for workers to transition into roles that offer greater purpose and satisfaction.

Accessibility Improvements

AI is also proving to be a game-changer in improving accessibility for people with disabilities and neurodivergent individuals. The innovations we're witnessing today go beyond leveling the playing field to unlock opportunities for greater independence and participation.

For example:

- **Assistive Devices:** Companies have developed eyeglasses that transcribe spoken words into text displayed directly in front of the wearer's face. This simple, yet transformative technology allows individuals who are deaf or hard of hearing to engage more easily in conversations and environments where sign language or written communication might not be practical.

- **Brain–Machine Interfaces:** Advances from companies like Neuralink are enabling individuals with paralysis to control devices such as computers or wheelchairs using neural signals. This technology restores a level of independence and mobility that was previously unimaginable.

Beyond these examples, AI-powered voice assistants, text-to-speech software, and adaptive technologies are breaking barriers for individuals across a spectrum of abilities. They enable participation in the workforce, education, and social activities, fostering a more inclusive society where everyone has the opportunity to contribute.

Environmental Protection

One of AI's most promising applications lies in protecting and preserving the environment. As the urgency of climate change grows, AI offers tools to monitor ecosystems, optimize resource use, and even predict natural disasters, enabling us to respond proactively.

Optimizing Conservation Efforts

AI can play a critical role in monitoring and protecting biodiversity. For example:

- **Ecosystem Monitoring:** AI systems can analyze satellite images to track deforestation, monitor wildlife populations, and detect illegal poaching activities in real time.
- **Predictive Modeling:** Machine learning algorithms can predict natural disasters like hurricanes or wildfires with greater accuracy, allowing communities to prepare and reduce damage.

Balancing Energy Demands

As industries and cities increasingly rely on AI for optimization, there's a clear tension: AI is energy-intensive, and its growing usage poses environmental challenges. However, this trade-off can be mitigated by the very breakthroughs that AI enables:

- **Energy Efficiency:** AI can optimize energy grids, reducing waste and improving distribution to meet demand with minimal environmental impact.
- **Clean Energy Innovation:** AI-powered simulations are helping scientists discover new materials for batteries and solar panels, paving the way for more sustainable energy storage and generation.

While the path forward requires careful consideration of energy consumption, the net impact of these advancements could be a more sustainable and resilient planet.

Empowering Everyone to Shape the Future

Realizing the full potential of these technologies requires diverse perspectives and collective action. The challenges discussed throughout this book—ethics, privacy, equitable access, and job transitions— cannot be solved in isolation or by technologists alone. To create an abundant future with AI, we need input from people across industries, socioeconomic backgrounds, and cultures.

I firmly believe in the power of collective knowledge and diverse thought. Whether you are a student, a factory worker, a CEO, or simply someone curious about how AI is changing the world, your voice matters. AI is not an isolated force; it is already woven into the fabric of our lives. By engaging with it thoughtfully and intentionally, we all have the opportunity to shape its trajectory.

This isn't just about technologists or policymakers. It's about everyone:

- Educators leveraging AI to personalize learning for students
- Farmers using AI to maximize crop yields sustainably
- Healthcare workers adopting AI tools to improve patient care

As we navigate this rapidly evolving landscape, I hope you feel empowered to take an active role in shaping the future. AI offers incredible opportunities, but it's up to us to ensure those opportunities are shared equitably and used ethically. By combining our unique experiences, skills, and perspectives, we can chart a course for a future that reflects our collective values and aspirations.

Whether you're improving your workflow with AI tools, advocating for responsible AI use, or pioneering innovations in your field, you are part of this journey. Together, we can ensure that AI serves as a force for good—one that enhances lives, protects the planet, and fosters a brighter, more inclusive future.

What Comes Next?

Throughout this book, we've explored the transformative power of AI, particularly generative AI, as it reshapes the way knowledge workers operate. However, as history has shown, technological advancements rarely pause to let the world catch up with them. The rapid acceleration of change that is occurring today compels us to look ahead and consider what lies on the horizon. To understand the future of work, I propose a framework based on three distinct epochs—periods marked by profound shifts in how humans and AI interact.

The rise of generative AI represents the beginning of a new epoch, redefining the nature of work, creativity, and collaboration. These epochs, which I call *Ask*, *Oversee*, and *Expansion*, map the journey from our current state to a transformative future where the boundaries between human and machine intelligence blur.

Epoch 1: Ask

The **Ask Epoch** is where we are now. It's a time when humans actively prompt AI systems to assist with tasks. This phase feels much like working with a smart, eager college intern. Generative AI today excels in providing insights, drafting content, debugging code, and much more. However, like an intern, it requires careful guidance, frequent corrections, and context-specific adjustments.

Characteristics of the Ask Epoch

Characteristics of the Ask Epoch include the following:

- **Prompting and Guidance:** Humans initiate tasks by asking specific questions or defining problems. The quality of outcomes depends on the clarity of the inputs.

- **Task Augmentation:** AI assists with repetitive or complex tasks, acting as a "second set of eyes" or an efficiency multiplier.

- **Adoption Challenges:** Individuals and organizations often struggle with identifying the right tasks to delegate to AI and adjusting workflows to incorporate these tools effectively.

Opportunities in the Ask Epoch

To fully embrace this phase, individuals and organizations must:

- **Document Workflows:** Analyze daily tasks to identify areas where AI tools can provide meaningful support.

- **Learn Prompting Skills:** Understanding how to communicate effectively with AI is a skill that can unlock its full potential.

- **Build Trust:** Trusting AI tools requires experimentation and familiarity. It's only through repeated use that individuals will feel confident relying on these systems.

Most knowledge workers and organizations will remain in this phase for the next five years, gradually adapting their workflows and building trust as they explore the capabilities of generative AI.

Epoch 2: Oversee

The **Oversee Epoch** represents the next major leap—a transition from actively prompting AI to overseeing its autonomous execution of tasks. In this phase, AI agents will gain the ability to move seamlessly across applications, perform sequences of tasks, and make decisions within predefined boundaries. Humans will step into the role of supervisors, monitoring the outcomes and providing strategic direction.

Characteristics of the Oversee Epoch

Characteristics of the Oversee Epoch will include the following:

- **Autonomous Task Execution:** AI agents handle entire workflows, from initiating a process to delivering the final result.

- **Tool Integration:** Software platforms integrate conversational AI capabilities, enabling tools to interact and collaborate autonomously.
- **Robotics Integration:** In blue-collar and manufacturing sectors, AI systems are embedded in robotic systems to perform tasks traditionally done by humans.

The Role of the Orchestrator

In this epoch, humans become conductors of the AI symphony:

- They set goals, define parameters, and monitor outcomes rather than performing tasks directly.
- They provide oversight, ensuring that AI-driven processes align with organizational objectives and ethical standards.

Opportunities and Challenges in the Oversee Epoch

While the Oversee Epoch promises significant growth and efficiency gains, it also comes with some notable risks:

- **Job Displacement:** The automation of complex workflows may lead to significant workforce transitions.
- **Accountability:** As AI agents take on more decision-making responsibilities, ensuring accountability and fairness becomes critical.
- **Ethical Navigation:** Balancing efficiency with ethical considerations will be paramount to avoid unintended consequences.

This epoch has the potential to bring unprecedented prosperity, but its success depends on careful navigation and inclusive strategies to mitigate disruption.

Epoch 3: Expansion

The **Expansion Epoch** represents the culmination of human–AI collaboration. In this phase, humans will integrate directly with AI systems to expand their cognitive and physical capabilities. This era, which is often referred to as the **Singularity**, envisions a future where the boundaries between biological and artificial intelligence dissolve.

Characteristics of the Expansion Epoch

Characteristics of the Expansion Epoch include the following:

- **Brain–Computer Interfaces (BCIs):** Companies like Neuralink are already developing technologies to connect human brains to computer systems, enabling seamless interaction with AI.

- **Exponential Intelligence:** By integrating with AI, humans could process information at speeds far beyond biological limitations, unlocking new levels of creativity, problem solving, and insight.

- **Co-creation:** This epoch heralds a new era of co-creation, where humans and AI work in tandem to push the boundaries of science, art, and technology.

Opportunities in the Expansion Epoch

The Expansion Epoch offers transformative possibilities:

- **Enhanced Learning:** Direct connections to AI systems could revolutionize education, allowing individuals to download and assimilate knowledge instantaneously.

- **Health and Longevity:** Integrated systems could monitor and optimize human health in real time, extending lifespans and improving quality of life.

- **Global Problem Solving:** AI–human integration could provide the computational power needed to address complex global challenges, from climate change to space exploration.

Ethical and Social Considerations

While the possibilities are exciting, this epoch also raises profound ethical questions:

- **Equity:** Who will have access to these capabilities, and how do we prevent widening socioeconomic disparities?

- **Identity:** What does it mean to be human when our cognitive processes are augmented by machines?

- **Autonomy:** As humans integrate with AI, ensuring autonomy and preserving individuality will be critical.

Predicted to emerge around 2045, this epoch heralds a profound transformation of what it means to be human.

Preparing for the Future

The journey through these epochs offers tremendous opportunities for growth, innovation, and creativity. However, realizing their full potential requires thoughtful planning, ethical navigation, and collective effort. As we transition from asking AI for help to overseeing its autonomous actions and eventually expanding our capabilities through integration, the role of humans will evolve from users to orchestrators to co-creators.

To thrive in this future, we must:

- **Adapt and Learn Continuously:** Each epoch will require new skills and mindsets, from effective prompting to strategic oversight to embracing technological augmentation.

- **Foster Inclusivity:** Ensuring equitable access to AI tools and technologies will be essential to avoid leaving marginalized communities behind.

- **Lead with Ethics:** As we shape this future, ethical considerations must guide every decision, from designing AI systems to integrating them into society.

By embracing these principles, we can navigate the coming epochs not as passive participants, but as active creators of a future defined by abundance, collaboration, and human ingenuity.

Navigating the Road Ahead

For many people, imagining a future where much of our work is handed over to machines, or a time when we connect our brains to the cloud to expand our intelligence, creates a profound sense of discomfort. This vision may evoke feelings of unease, fear of the unknown, or questions about what it means to be human in the AI age. But I assure you, not only will we welcome these changes, but we will ease into them naturally, just as we have done with countless technological advancements in the past.

A Story of Everyday Augmentation

Last night, as I tended to my plants, I realized one needed repotting. Without hesitation, I ordered new potting soil and a planter on Amazon at 9:00 PM. The next morning, by 10:00 AM, the package was on my doorstep. Inside were exactly the items I'd envisioned less than 24 hours earlier. This is such a commonplace occurrence today that we rarely stop to marvel at it. But imagine telling this story to someone living 100 years ago: They would be astonished.

Their amazement wouldn't just be about the speed of delivery. They would wonder at the logistics: How could you possibly find the exact pot you needed without leaving your house? How could it arrive so quickly?

And wouldn't such convenience come at a staggering cost? To their surprise, you could explain that many goods obtained this way are not just cheaper than what's available in local stores, but more accessible than crafting them by hand or sourcing them from specialty merchants.

This seamless interaction, enabled by algorithms that suggest the perfect products, logistics systems that optimize warehouse operations, and delivery systems that bring goods to your door, is powered by AI. Just as this process has become a mundane part of our lives, so too will more advanced AI systems become integrated into our daily routines. What may seem extraordinary or even intimidating now will soon become ordinary and widely embraced.

The Gradual Transition

Technological change has always been accompanied by skepticism and wonder. Fifty years ago, people marveled at computers that could fill an entire room. Today, we carry devices in our pockets that are exponentially more powerful, yet we think little of their impact on our lives. Similarly, the AI systems we marvel at today will soon become the everyday tools of tomorrow.

Children born today will likely graduate college at a time when augmenting human intelligence through AI is as common as using the Internet is now. Indeed, you might find yourself explaining to your grandchildren how you had to manually search for information using tools like Google and Wikipedia. They might laugh at how slow and inefficient those methods seem compared to the instant, brain-integrated access they'll enjoy. What feels like science fiction now will become a natural part of the human experience.

You, Augmented

To envision the future, imagine yourself as an augmented version of who you are today. In many ways, this future is already here. Consider how much you rely on the technology in your pocket—that is, your smartphone. With it, you navigate the world without paper maps, relying instead on GPS with voice commands. You have a near-infinite library of knowledge at your fingertips, accessible through search engines and apps. You use this small device to stay connected, solve problems, and manage your daily life.

These tools have already augmented your capabilities, though they may not feel extraordinary because we've quickly adapted to their presence.

This is the pattern of technological progress: What feels revolutionary today becomes routine tomorrow.

As AI continues to evolve, this augmentation will extend beyond external devices to our own minds. Imagine the possibilities:

- **Enhanced Creativity:** What could you create if you had instant access to computational power within your own brain? Could you write novels, direct films, or compose symphonies that have always existed in your imagination but were limited by technical barriers?

- **Multifaceted Careers:** Would you take on a day job but also pursue passions like art, music, or entrepreneurship on the side, leveraging AI to handle the technical aspects while you focus on vision and creativity?

- **Limitless Learning:** Could you master new languages, explore complex scientific theories, or understand different cultures in ways that currently require years of study?

This future isn't just about efficiency; it's about unlocking human potential in ways we can only begin to imagine.

How to Adapt

Adapting to this future doesn't require extraordinary technical skills. It starts with curiosity—a willingness to explore, test new tools, and expand your thinking about what is possible. Here are a few practical steps to help you navigate this journey.

Embrace Experimentation

One of the greatest barriers to progress is the fear of failure. Start small by experimenting with AI tools that can streamline your daily tasks, whether by generating ideas, managing schedules, or automating repetitive processes. Each experiment will build familiarity and trust.

Rethink Focus and Productivity

Studies show that most individuals achieve a scant 2–4 hours of high-quality focus during a typical 8-hour workday. By leveraging AI to handle routine or time-consuming tasks, you can reserve your focus for work that truly matters. Use tools like AI scheduling assistants or generative AI platforms to reduce mental clutter and free up cognitive bandwidth.

Redefine Collaboration

Recognize that AI is a collaborator, not a competitor. Treat it as an extension of your team, capable of handling repetitive tasks while you focus on strategic decision making, innovation, and human connection.

Stay Curious and Open-Minded

The rapid pace of technological change means that adaptability is more important than expertise. Stay curious, keep learning, and remain open to new possibilities. Your willingness to evolve will be your greatest asset.

A Future of Creation

The road ahead is paved with opportunity; it should not be viewed as a source of fear. As we lean into the AI-augmented future, we should stop worrying about what we might lose and begin imagining what we can create. By embracing these tools as partners, we open the door to a world where human creativity, intelligence, and ingenuity are amplified in ways never seen before.

So, take a moment to imagine your future self—a self not limited by the tools of today, but rather empowered by the limitless possibilities of tomorrow. What will you create? How will you grow? The answers lie in your willingness to embrace change and become an active participant in shaping what comes next.

Embrace Your Role as the Orchestrator

While I wish I could provide you with a definitive list of every job that will emerge in this new technological revolution and a detailed roadmap for the skills you should master, doing so would rob you of the rewards and lessons from the journey. The beauty of this moment in history lies in its openness, the potential for each of us to carve our own path and shape the future in ways that are uniquely ours.

To navigate and thrive in this era of transformation, you don't need to predict every change. Instead, you need to tap into your curiosity, focus on what genuinely excites you, and thoughtfully consider how you want to augment yourself. Most importantly, *start small*. As someone who has coached many individuals entering data science and AI, I've seen people stumble by trying to learn everything at once, juggling multiple

programming languages, signing up for countless classes, and ultimately feeling overwhelmed. True progress comes not from quantity but from focus and application.

Here are a few simple principles to guide your journey, no matter how you choose to adapt and grow.

Be Curious and Look for Inspiration

We live in an age of unprecedented access to information and inspiration. Explore platforms like LinkedIn, Instagram, X (formerly Twitter), and news outlets for real-world applications of AI that ignite your interest. From advancements in healthcare to creative uses in art, there's a wealth of innovation waiting to be discovered.

Once you find an area that intrigues you, *dive in deeply*. Use AI tools to help you explore using AI to learn about AI (yes, this is meta, but that's the point). Tools like ChatGPT, Khanmigo, and other AI tutors can serve as personalized guides, offering tailored explanations and instant feedback. Don't just consume knowledge; engage with it. Ask questions, test ideas, and let your curiosity guide you.

Focus and Deepen Your Knowledge

As you explore, you'll inevitably uncover a multitude of interesting paths. The challenge is to resist spreading yourself too thin. Instead, *narrow your focus* and commit to deepening your understanding in one area.

This doesn't mean avoiding other opportunities. Instead, it means diving deeply enough to gain mastery before you branch out. Retake classes to solidify your foundation, consult AI tools for clarification, and, most importantly, apply what you're learning. Whether through personal projects, professional applications, or community initiatives, practice transforms knowledge into skill.

Experiment and Embrace Failure

True growth comes from experimentation. Test your ideas, try new tools, and don't shy away from mistakes. Every failure is a step toward refinement and understanding.

This mindset isn't just about personal growth; it's about pushing boundaries. We need individuals from diverse backgrounds and experiences to bring fresh perspectives to this space. The more you experiment and test new capabilities, the more you'll uncover unexpected opportunities and solutions.

By *embracing failure*, you don't just adapt to change–you become a leader, someone who inspires others to step into the unknown with courage and curiosity.

Orchestrating Your Future

Now is the time to step into your role as an orchestrator—not just of your life, but of your team, organization, and community. It's a testament to human ingenuity that we've created tools capable of continually expanding our civilization. This moment invites you to harness those tools, not passively, but with purpose and vision.

For an AI Orchestrator, the quest involves more than simply obtaining skills. You've played the instruments, studied the music, and learned the craft. Now, your task is to shape the symphony—a symphony that reflects your unique perspective, your passions, and your vision for the future.

Working alongside AI doesn't diminish our humanity; it amplifies it. AI provides the tools, the extra hands, the computational power to help us dream bigger, create faster, and solve problems more effectively. But the soul of the work, the creativity, the empathy, the vision, remains human.

Take a moment to imagine the symphony you want to conduct:

• What do you want to create?
• How do you want to contribute?
• What impact do you hope to leave behind?

This is your time to dream boldly and act decisively. The tools are here. The possibilities are endless. All that's needed is your curiosity, focus, and willingness to create.

You have within you the power to focus, the ability to learn and adapt, and the imagination to create. By embracing curiosity, committing to lifelong learning, and taking intentional steps forward, you're not just keeping up with change–you're shaping it.

This is your moment to lead. Take up these tools, orchestrate your symphony, and create the reality you've envisioned. Together, we can craft a future defined not by fear of change but by the boundless opportunities it brings.

Bibliography

Chapter 1

Bezjak, S., et al. (2018). *Open Science Training Handbook*.

Biermann, O. C., et al. (2022). From Tool to Companion: Storywriters Want AI Writers to Respect Their Personal Values and Writing Strategies. *Proceedings of the 2022 ACM Designing Interactive Systems Conference* (DIS '22).

Brynjolfsson, E., et al. (2023). Generative AI at Work. NBER Working Paper 31161.

Dell'Acqua, F., et al. (2023). Navigating the Jagged Technological Frontier: Field Experimental Evidence of the Effects of AI on Knowledge Worker Productivity and Quality. SSRN Working Paper 4573321.

Haslberger, M., et al. (2023). No Great Equalizer: Experimental Evidence on AI in the UK Labor Market. SSRN Working Paper 4594466.

Kneupper, C. W. (1978). Teaching Argument: An Introduction to the Toulmin Model. *College Composition and Communication*, 29, 3.

Lee, M., et al. (2022). CoAuthor: Designing a Human–AI Collaborative Writing Dataset for Exploring Language Model Capabilities. *Proceedings of the 2022 CHI Conference on Human Factors in Computing Systems*.

Lee, S., et al. (2023). Fostering Youth's Critical Thinking Competency About AI Through Exhibition. *Proceedings of the 2023 CHI Conference on Human Factors in Computing Systems*.

LinkedIn. (2023). *Future of Work Report: AI at Work*.

Mollick, E. (2023). My Class Required AI. Here's What I've Learned So Far. *One Useful Thing*. www.oneusefulthing.org/p/my-class-required-ai-heres-what-ive

Noy, S., and Zhang, W. (2023). Experimental Evidence on the Productivity Effects of Generative Artificial Intelligence. SSRN Working Paper 4375283.

Peng, S., et al. (2023). The Impact of AI on Developer Productivity: Evidence from GitHub Copilot. https://arxiv.org/abs/2302.06590

Sarkar, A. (2023). Exploring Perspectives on the Impact of Artificial Intelligence on the Creativity of Knowledge Work: Beyond Mechanised Plagiarism and Stochastic Parrots. *Proceedings of the ACM*.

Spatharioti, S. E., et al. (2023). Comparing Traditional and LLM-Based Search for Consumer Choice: A Randomized Experiment. https://arxiv.org/abs/2307.03744

Sun, N., et al. (2017). Critical Thinking in Collaboration: Talk Less, Perceive More. *Proceedings of the 2017 CHI Conference Extended Abstracts on Human Factors in Computing Systems*.

Symposium on Human–Computer Interaction for Work. (CHIWORK 2023).

Toner-Rodgers, Aidan. (2024). Artificial Intelligence, Scientific Discovery, and Product Innovation. https://arxiv.org/abs/2412.17866

Chapter 2

Battle, Rick, and Teja Gollapudi. (2024). The Unreasonable Effectiveness of Eccentric Automatic Prompts. https://arxiv.org/pdf/2402.10949.pdf

Claude3. Prompt Engineering Overview. https://docs.anthropic.com/claude/docs/prompt-engineering/

IQ Scores by Profession. https://gitnux.org/average-iq-by-profession/

Roivainen, Eka. (2023). I Gave ChatGPT an IQ Test. Here's What I Discovered. https://www.scientificamerican.com/article/i-gave-chatgpt-an-iq-test-heres-what-i-discovered/

Sahoo, P., et al. (2025). A Systematic Survey of Prompt Engineering in Large Language Models: Techniques and Applications. https://arxiv.org/pdf/2402.07927.pdf

Chapter 3

Buhler, Konstantine. (2023). AI and the Frontier Paradox. https://www.sequoiacap.com/article/ai-paradox-perspective/

Longman Dictionary of Contemporary English. "artificial intelligence." https://www.ldoceonline.com/dictionary/artificial-intelligence

Manning, Christopher. (2020). Artificial Intelligence Definitions. https://hai.stanford.edu/sites/default/files/2020-09/AI-Definitions-HAI.pdf

Chapter 5

Microsoft and LinkedIn. (2024). 2024 Work Trend Index Annual Report. https://www.microsoft.com/en-us/worklab/work-trend-index/ai-at-work-is-here-now-comes-the-hard-part?utm_source=newsletter.ai-academy.com&utm_medium=newsletter&utm_campaign=openai-and-google-battle-over-smartest-ai-assistant

Chapter 6

Anthropic. (2024). Mapping the Mind of a Large Language Model. https://www.anthropic.com/news/mapping-mind-language-model

Longman Dictionary of Contemporary English. "ethic." https://www.ldoceonline.com/dictionary/ethic#google_vignette

Luccioni, Alexandra Sasha, et al. (2024). Power Hungry Processing: Watts Driving the Cost of AI Deployment? https://arxiv.org/pdf/2311.16863

Model Hallucination Leaderboard. https://github.com/vectara/hallucination-leaderboard

Nicoletti, Leonardo, and Dina Bass. (2023). Humans Are Biased. Generative AI Is Even Worse. https://www.bloomberg.com/graphics/2023-generative-ai-bias/

Turner Lee, Nicol, et al. (2019). Algorithmic Bias Detection and Mitigation: Best Practices and Policies to Reduce Consumer Harms. https://www.brookings.edu/articles/algorithmic-bias-detection-and-mitigation-best-practices-and-policies-to-reduce-consumer-harms/

Chapter 7

Willige, Andrea, and Gayle Markovitz. (2023). The Future of Jobs: Two Experts Explain How Technology Is Transforming Almost Every Task. https://www.weforum.org/agenda/2023/05/future-of-jobs-technology-skills-workplace/

Index